Comedia Series ● 28

FOURTH-RATE ESTATE:

An Anatomy of Fleet Street

by Tom Baistow

Comedia Publishing Group
9 Poland Street, London W1V 3DG

D0351228

Comedia Publishing Group was set up to investigate and monitor the media in Britain and abroad. The aim of the project is to provide basic information, investigate problem areas, and to share the experiences of those working in the field, while encouraging debate about the future development of the media. The opinions expressed in the books in the Comedia series are those of the authors, and do not necessarily reflect the views of Comedia.

For a list of other Comedia titles see back pages.

First published in 1985 by Comedia Publishing Group

ISBN 0 906 890 829 (paperback)
ISBN 0 906 890 837 (hardback)

British Library Cataloguing in Publication Data

Tom Baistow
  1. Fourth Rate Estate: Anatomy of Fleet Street
  I. Title
  072′. PN5118

Cover design by Peter Baistow

Typeset by Photosetting, 6 Foundry House, Stars Lane, Yeovil, Somerset BA20 1NL. Tel. (0935) 23684

Printed by Unwin Brothers Ltd
The Gresham Press, Old Woking, Surrey

Trade Distribution by Comedia, 9 Poland Street, London W1

Distributed in Australia by Second Back Row Press
50 Govett St. Katoomba, N.S.W. 2780

Distributed in Canada: 229 College Street, Toronto
Ontario, Canada M5T 1R4

Acknowledgements

It is a measure of the sensitivities that prevail in Fleet Street, whose business is to disclose and expose, that my sources there prefer to remain anonymous in the interests of industrial peace and personal relations. My sincere thanks to them, nonetheless, for giving me generously of their valuable time and so much inside information that normally does not get into print. I would like to record my indebtedness to: Clive Thornton, former chairman-designate of Mirror Group Newspapers for his help; and Frank Allaun for kindly providing me with Dr. Jörg Soehring's notes on Right of Reply practice in Germany. My thanks, also, to MEAL (Media Expenditure Analysis Limited) for making available to me the statistics quoted in Chapter 3 and to JICNARS for affording me access to its National Readership Survey.

As with all such eclectic studies, this one owes much to previous labourers in the EC4 vineyard, some of whose works are listed in the bibliography, as well as innumerable fellow journalists whose experiences are integral to the story. Not least, I wish to thank Charles Landry for inviting me to write the book.

For Mae

Contents

Foreword

At a point in the Thatcherisation of Britain when the Prime Minister,
in her latest manifestation as editor-in-chief of the nation's news
media, has decreed, in another of her copywriter's purple PR phrases,
that it is their duty to deny terrorists the 'oxygen of publicity', when
her Home Secretary, in his disingenuous guise as An Average Viewer,
Whitehall, SW1, has at a stroke compromised the BBC's credibility at
home and, above all, abroad, the need is greater than ever for an
independent, disinterested, fair and diverse press to defend the
complete freedom of expression that newspapers rightly demand for
themselves.

  It would be rash indeed to underestimate the influence of
television as a mass medium, but its very strengths, immediacy and
the dramatic element in 'live' coverage, point up the transitory and
insubstantial nature of its essentially pictorial message. It is the
printed word, with its unlimited capacity for comprehensive
investigation of a situation and the detailed unravelling of complex
issues beyond the scope of the oral bulletin, its unrivalled quality as a
forum in which ideas can be exchanged and pros and cons set out and
argued, its durability as a record of what people say and do, its
flexibility as a pocket medium that can be carried about and kept to
be read and re-read at will, that in the final analysis must be the most
important safeguard of the democratic process.

  But what kind of press have we got? And how does it use its
freedom? For one thing, it is overwhelmingly Tory – 11 of the 17

national newspapers follow the Conservative line. For another, it is dominated by a handful of millionaire businessmen: three entre-preneurs control 10 papers that have 80 per cent of the market in readership terms, papers that faithfully reflect the personal views and commercial interests of their owners. At opposite ends of the editorial spectrum Murdoch's once-great *Times* and Maxwell's once-radical *Mirror* have both come out against the BBC's claim for an increase in the television licence fee: *The Times* has even advocated that the Corporation, until now regarded abroad as the independent and impartial voice of Britain, should be broken up. The proprietors of both papers have extensive holdings in alternative commercial television systems such as cable which hope to woo viewers from the two established networks – a task that would be demonstrably easier if the BBC were to be privatised in line with Conservative ideology. Further, the very tabloids which cry 'Hands off the freedom of the press – no censorship!' when their more outrageous excesses provoke a call for more effective sanctions than Press Council censure, enthusiastically approved the Home Secretary's intervention in the BBC's editorial decision-making. As Murdoch's *Sun* put it, without batting an eyelid, when the BBC declared that it had a duty to maintain balance in its programmes: 'What wicked nonsense. There is no "balance" between good and evil...'

Balance is hardly a concept on which the tit-and-trash press can be said to pronounce with authority. The heavy slanting of the BBC story is merely the latest example in a continuing process of exaggerating, distorting and colouring what little real news the down-market papers cram in between the endless columns of sensation and trivia. The ordinary man and woman, it is often claimed, don't believe all they read in the papers. Yet 85 per cent of them buy tabloids, and it is axiomatic that some mud always sticks – not least the kind of mud dredged up from the gutter by junk journalism. For that reason the chapters of this book which deal with the purely editorial aspects of the newspaper industry focus largely on the behaviour and methods of the popular press. This is not to imply that the so-called qualities are beyond criticism. But for the A, B, C1 readership classes, at least, there is an element of choice. Even if there is no socialist voice as such among the serious papers there are two dailies of contrasting political outlook but which share one important distinction that marks them out from the rest of the national quality press – both are entirely independent of conglomerate backing and the axe-grinding that comes with such support: the *Guardian*, which is controlled by the Scott Trust, easily the best-written of the heavies, whose remarkable rise in circulation, without any artificial aids such as *The Times*'s genteel up-market version of bingo, testifies to the excellence of its wide-ranging coverage of every field from politics to sport, not forgetting feminism, and its commendably liberal, broadminded appeal to the thinking Left and Centre; and Lord Hartwell's *The Daily Telegraph*, whose Conservative stance – not always in concert with the Downing Street lined toed so slavishly by its tabloid fellow Tories – is neutralised for many non-believers by what is undoubtedly the most comprehensive and, on the whole, reasonably impartial news service of any British paper, even if its austerely grey columns lack the *Guardian*'s stylistic panache.

It is the unreal economics of the national press that have made the very independence from commercial conglomerates enjoyed by the trust-controlled *Guardian* and the family-owned *Telegraphs* the rare exceptions to the rule as a new breed of self-made tycoons has moved in, cash in hand, to take over long-established newspapers as if they were High Street drapery stores. As this book goes to press, United Newspapers plc, owner of the *Yorkshire Post* and *Punch* among many other publications, is beginning its battle to secure control of Lord Matthews's Fleet Holdings and its three newspapers, the *Daily Express*, *Sunday Express* and *Daily Star*, which only became independent of their Trafalgar House parent group in 1982. Public companies like Fleet and Mirror Group Newspapers – when controlled by Reed International – are obviously vulnerable to the shareholder-bribing technique, but family ownership is no guarantee of continuing independence when a paper depends entirely on the money it makes from selling papers and when the books get too red for the family's comfort.

In 1960, after losses of £300,000 that year, the Daily News Trust, controlled by the Cadbury family, the multi-millionaire confectionery magnates, delivered the liberal *News Chronicle* into the arms of its political opponent, Lord Rothermere's fiercely Tory *Daily Mail*, for the sum of £1.9m. The late Gavin (later Lord) Astor, who recently died a multi-millionaire, sold *The Times* to Roy Thomson in 1966 when it made its first post-war loss – a paltry £250,000 – and his cousin, David Astor, handed over the no less prestigious *Observer* for a nominal sum to the American oil giant Atlantic Richfield in 1976 when the family trust decided it could no longer fund its mounting losses. In the same year the late Sir Max Aitken sold his debt-ridden Beaverbrook Newspapers, which had always relied solely on the income from newspaper sales, to Trafalgar House. Even the solid-looking *Telegraph*'s future has become the subject of speculation since it went to the market this summer to raise the £110m it needs for the development of its new dockland printing plant and long-overdue modernisation – and found that Conrad Black, a Canadian multi-millionaire entrepreneur with newspaper interests, had bought 14 per cent of the shares and a non-executive directorship for £10m. If the *Telegraph* were to find itself in financial trouble, runs the speculation, would Hartwell or his heirs sell out, and to whom – Black, another Canadian like Beaverbrook and Thomson?

The national press's inherent financial instability – for which the unions must shoulder their not inconsiderable share of the blame – has been the prime factor in the concentration of ownership, the polarisation between a minority of quality papers and the mass circulation tabloids and the depressing drop in journalistic standards. It is the story Fleet Street doesn't print. I hope that this book will help to throw some light on a problem for our kind of society that transcends Fleet Street's self-interest and, perhaps, encourage wider discussion of potential paths to a healthy pluralist press.

Tom Baistow
August, 1985

Chapter 1

Whose freedom of the press?

*Newspapers are unique barometers of their age. They indicate
more plainly than anything else the climate of the societies to
which they belong.*

– Francis Williams

Of all the stale traditional myths that mask the sombre realities in Mrs
Thatcher's Britain, from the vaunted superiority of the 'Mother of
Parliaments' over lesser legislatures to the unrivalled fairness of
British justice, none is more anachronistically corrosive than the
legend – sedulously promoted by newspapers themselves at any sign
of a threat to their 'independence', piously lip-served by every
government since the war, sanctified by successive Royal Commissions and actively fostered by the education system – that the British
press is truly free and that its freedom is the guarantee of our liberty,
personal and national, the very bulwark of democracy: the legend
that the Fourth Estate, as Fleet Street persists in calling itself, is the
fearless defender of the public interest, eternally vigilant in the
pursuit of truth, the exposure of corruption and the abuse of power.

Sadly, in the face of the challenges that confront Britain, the
urgent need to bridge the debilitating divisions of its Them and Us –
North and South society, to adapt its deeply engrained mores to the
social and industrial problems of the microelectronic age in a highly
competitive world and, not least, to combat the creeping encroach-
ment on its hard-won civil liberties, the Establishment legend is a
cynical caricature of the real nature of the present-day national press.
When Macaulay declared, 157 years ago, that 'the gallery in which the
reporters sit has become a fourth estate of the realm', newspapers
were emerging from two centuries of repressive laws, financial
corruption and political bribery, and a new breed of independent,
campaigning editors of the stature of Thomas Barnes of *The Times*
and William Cobbett of *The Political Register* had initiated the great
debate that led to the Reform Bill of 1832 and the long struggle for
political and social justice.

Today their successors preside over a Fourth-Rate Estate, largely
devoted to junk journalism in the pursuit of circulation at any price

and the continuance in power of a party that represents only a minority of the electorate but an overwhelming majority of newspaper proprietors. Today the British read more newspapers proportionally than any comparable Western nation* and most of them read some of the trashiest, most politically partisan papers in the world – half a dozen mass circulation tabloids, dailies and Sundays, which have brought British journalism down to the level of the sex and crime pulp magazine, exploiting the sensational and the trivial at the expense of the significant, substituting soft porn for hard news and technical slickness for professional integrity, unashamedly pushing their owners' commercial interests while soft-pedalling their more controversial activities, distorting the facts of the political scene by biased selection, suppression and character assassination, desperately trying to inflate their circulations by bigger and bigger bingo prizes, flaunting their contempt for the impotent censure of the Press Council, refusing redress to those they have misreported, misrepresented or maligned. While it is happily true that a handful of quality papers are among the best in the world, combining high journalistic standards with editorial balance, whatever their politics, it is also depressingly true that their total circulations add up to a mere 15 per cent of the nationals' total sales.

The real freedom of the press in this country has long been the freedom of millionaires, whatever their backgrounds or countries of origin, to buy themselves newspapers that will propagate their views. But at least there was a modifying diversity among previous press barons that made for a more heterogeneous national press, in terms of both editorial standards and political viewpoints. Today the concentration of ownership has reached near-monopoly and a new breed of tycoon has moved into the seats of editorial power. Seven men, four of them entrepreneurs who have risen to commercial power in the wheeler-dealer world of the takeover, now control no fewer than 16 of the 17 national papers, with 97 per cent of the daily market and 100 per cent of Sunday sales:

Rupert Murdoch (*The Times*, *Sunday Times*, *Sun* and *News of the World*); Robert Maxwell (*The Mirror*, *Sunday Mirror*, *Sunday People*, plus the *Glasgow Daily Record*, *Sunday Mail* and the racing daily *Sporting Life*); Lord (Victor) Matthews (*Daily Express*, *Daily Star* and *Sunday Express*, plus joint control of the *London Standard*, five provincial papers and Morgan Grampian magazines); Viscount Rothermere (*Daily Mail*, *Mail on Sunday*, plus 32 provincial papers including 14 dailies); Lord Hartwell (*Daily Telegraph*, *Sunday*

---

* See table on p. 7

Telegraph); Viscount Cowdray (*Financial Times*, plus the Pearson/ Westminster Press group of 103 provincial papers, including two dailies and ten evenings); and Roland (Tiny) Rowland (*Observer*, plus *Glasgow Herald*, two Scottish evenings and 18 weeklies). Alone of all the nationals, the *Guardian* is not controlled by a single boss, whether parvenu tycoon or press baron's heir, like Rothermere and Hartwell, but governed by the non-profit-making Scott Trust.

Two of the new breed of press barons, Maxwell and Rowland, have tarnished business reputations; two of them, Murdoch and Rothermere, a tax exile, are in effect absentee landlords who seldom visit this country; and three of them, Murdoch, Maxwell and Rowland, acquired their newspapers in deals which, in terms of that all-purpose Fleet Street cliché, 'the public interest', left a lot to be desired. And all of them are men of the Right with the single exception of Maxwell, who combines his proclaimed support for Labour with a declared admiration for Mrs Thatcher, and sees no conflict between the extravert patriotism of his *Mirror* slogan, 'Forward with Britain', and the prudent siting of its parent company in tight little Liechtenstein, haven of international capital. Hardly the praetorian guard that a well-balanced democracy might choose to protect the integrity of the printed word and the wells of truth. But if the hard core of the new race of proprietors reflects the predatory, money-fixated ethos of the current Conservative brand of free-wheeling capitalism, Fleet Street's myriad chapels present the no less questionable obverse of the coin, the unprepossessing face of a greedy, anarchic trade unionism which cynically exploits the power of the closed shop to press its – often inordinate – claims with damaging stoppages in an industry whose product is the most perishable of all – news. Both sides of the industry may, poetically, deserve each other, but by any democratic test the reading public deserves better than the sum of their sectarian interests provides.

The national press has never reflected the political attitudes of a large – often a major – sector of the population in any representative degree since the rise of the Labour party after the 1914-18 war, but at least there was a greater choice of newspapers, with a wider diversity of editorial views and generally a less crudely partisan approach to the selection and treatment of news, before and just after the second world war, when the Conservative and Labour parties alternated in government.

Today the concentration of ownership in right-wing hands compounds the blatant inequity of an outmoded electoral system which in 1983 gave an overwhelming majority of more than 140 seats to a Tory government returned by only 30 per cent of the electorate. This at a time when the shift of power from the floor of the Commons to the executive has increased sharply under a dominating prime minister bent on centralising control, political, administrative and fiscal; at a time when her obsessively secretive government has no compunction in resorting to the long-discredited Official Secrets Act to cover shifty ministerial manoeuvres, while sparing no efforts to manage the news, through press and broadcasting, and no expense in projecting her Saatchi & Saatchi image. In short, the dice in both Westminster and Fleet Street are now heavily loaded against the 29 million who did not vote Tory at the last election, the real silent majority, by the mutually profitable nature of the implicit contract between the Third and Fourth Estates.

Leader writers never tire of quoting Delane's dictum, that the business of the press is to disclose, whenever their newspapers unearth – or, more frequently, a mole presents them with – the makings of a good scandal, preferably one in a nationalised industry, a trade union, the BBC, a Labour council or the NHS. 'No effort must be spared to ensure that the full story of the corruption and mismanagement is made public and the offenders rigorously dealt with ...' – the blend of self-righteous moralising and minatory comment may reek of hypocrisy, yet the watchdog role, however selectively played, however partisan, remains a basic function of the press. The one scandal the press never blows the gaff on, however, is the real state of Fleet Street itself – that stays discreetly undisclosed in a classic Catch-22 trap which keeps the great mass of readers undisturbed by revelations about the undemocratic nature of newspaper ownership and editorial control and the corrupt character of overpaid, overmanned and underemployed chapels whose bizarre practices make the 'Car workers who sleep on night-shift' of the scathing tabloid exposés look like Stakhanovites. The only medium that could tell all and do the story justice is the newspaper industry itself, but dog doesn't eat dog in Fleet Street: the central doctrine of the 'free press', the divine right of powerful individuals to control newspapers and decide what goes – and what does not go – in them is never questioned. Occasionally one dog may snarl at another, as when the *Sun* accused the *Mirror* of treason for not joining the other tabloids in their orgy of jingoism during the Falklands campaign; or lift a hind leg to pour scorn or squirt malice on a rival, as when the *Mirror* attacked the *Sun* for plagiarism because it 'stole' several of its laughably lightweight 'exclusives' about pop stars earlier this year (the 'lifting' of other papers' stories after the first editions have appeared is as traditional a practice as the naïve psychological ploy of putting an 'exclusive' label on a hyped-up version of PR background material and cafe gossip available to any paper at the lower end of the market).

The qualities may sniff at the tabloids' bingo antics and condemn their more outrageous excesses as they battle to secure the memoirs of mass murderers and gangsters' girl friends (although *The Times* and *Sunday Times*, once so critical of gutter journalism, have become noticeably broadminded about such vulgar goings-on since Mr Murdoch made them bedfellows of the *Sun* and *News of the World*) but they too steer well clear of the basic questions that would lead to trouble with either their owners or the unions who set, print and distribute newspapers. For obvious reasons. For one thing, proprietors choose editors they know will toe their line.

The modern concept of editorial independence was defined perfectly in a memorable obiter dictum by Victor Matthews when Trafalgar House won the auction for the Express group in 1977: 'By and large, the editors will have complete freedom as long as they agree with the policy I have laid down'. There are honourable, if rare, exceptions to the Matthews rule. The editor of the *Observer*, Donald Trelford, who was appointed by the paper's former trustees in consultation with the editorial staff ten years ago, long before it was taken over by Tiny Rowland, courageously defied his proprietor's wishes last year in a widely publicised slanging match, and personally reported and published the Mugabe government's brutal campaign against the Matabeleland 'dissidents' in Zimbabwe, where Rowland's Lonrho group has highly profitable commercial interests. Trelford risked not only his job but the closure of the paper – Lonrho underwrites the *Observer's* losses – to assert his independence. Peter Preston of the *Guardian*, who also was appointed by a panel of trustees, with staff representation, enjoys probably the greatest freedom of any modern editor, in the paper's long liberal tradition. On the Right, William Deedes edits the *Daily Telegraph* with the assured authority of a former Conservative minister of independent mind, working in close tandem with his proprietor and editor-in-chief, Lord Hartwell, himself a lifelong active newspaperman. And the *Financial Time's* independent line, refreshingly nonconformist on the larger issues for a City paper, underlines that its editor, Geoffrey Owen, is his own man in the *FT* tradition.

But these exceptions merely highlight the drastic decline in the editor's status and authority since the first quarter of the century when a man of the calibre of A J Spender, of the (Liberal) *Westminster Gazette*, refused to print even letters to the editor from its owner, Sir Alfred Mond, founder of ICI and later Lord Melchett, because, as he explained, his readers would not like such signs of personal interference in matters of policy. Spender went on to edit the paper for 26 years. On some of today's tabloids – Lord Matthews's for example – the editor is lucky to last 26 months.

In the classic tradition that was one of the casualties of the Northcliffe revolution, proprietors enjoyed the social and political cachet and the profits, if any, or the privilege of paying the bills, while their editors enjoyed the freedom, and responsibility, of deciding policy that gave the national press a healthy pluralism offering the reader a wide choice. Today the message is pre-programmed, the medium another extension of its owner's pursuit of power. Editors are hired, not for their public reputation as informed commentators on the issues of the day, social campaigners, critics of society, citizens of the wider cosmos with a deep knowledge of national and international affairs, but for their technical expertise in the packaging and presentation of a magazine-type formula, their professional ability to find the right slot in a grossly overcrowded market, and they are fired as unceremoniously as football managers when they fail to produce the magic recipe that will at last win enough circulation, and therefore advertising, for the paper at least to break even – and few of them consistently do so.

At the root of this editorial instability, the press's moral malaise and the vulnerability of long-established papers to take-over by outsiders of doubtful repute are a ramshackle financial structure whose overdependence on advertising revenue exposes it to every economic ill wind, and unsophisticated management that is the prisoner of Lewis Carroll industrial custom and usage, and top-heavy overheads that are the unions' blackmail price of uninterrupted production. By its very nature Fleet Street is the perfect jungle for self-made predators willing to fork out some of their conglomerates' money to acquire the influence and prestige – or at least the publicity that passes for prestige in the nouveau riche layer of big business – deemed to go with ownership of a newspaper, however down-market; a useful machine for laundering personal and company reputations as well as advancing the cause of 'free' enterprise – and, eventually, when little local peccadilloes have been given the Soviet Encyclo-paedia treatment by time and tame biographers, advancing the chances of a grateful government of either complexion making one a real armigerous press baron ... 'M'lords, ladies, gentlemen and his millions of readers, pray silence for the Right Honourable the Lord Copper of Fleet Ditch in the City of London'.

That is the real chequebook journalism that will have to be tackled if the freedom of the press is ever to become more than a sanitising cliché – the frenetic scramble to get in the right bid before the inevitable queue of equally sharp rivals, using every trick in the takeover book, to get hold of one's own newspaper. As a study of recent Fleet Street takeovers will show, the new generation of press barons have nothing to learn from their journalist employees who fought – sometimes physically – and intrigued with such professional dedication to secure their 'exclusive inside story' of the Yorkshire Ripper's bloody route to front-page fame.

The newspaper habit: an international table circulation per 1,000 inhabitants	
Sweden	526
UK	479
Norway	456
Denmark	367
Netherlands	325
W. Germany	324
US	282
France	238
Italy	97

Source: United Nations Yearbook

Chapter 2

Predators in the paper jungle

None can love freedom heartily but good men; the rest love not freedom, but licence.

– John Milton

The precarious tenure of editors is both a yardstick of Fleet Street's inherent instability and a reflection of proprietorial impotence when faced with its basic problem: the national press, as presently constituted, is in real terms a shrinking industry, and the only way a paper can expand is by taking readers from another paper. The present editor of Lord Matthews's *Daily Express*, Larry (Sir Albert) Lamb, is the twelfth to occupy the paper's chair in the 28 years since the retirement of the legendary Arthur Christiansen, who pushed its sales up to $4\frac{1}{2}$ million during his 23 years as Lord Beaverbrook's editorial technician-in-chief; his successors have averaged two years and four months in office as sales have slumped to below two million. Lamb, at the time of writing, has been editing the *Express* for exactly two years, but the paper's circulation has actually fallen, for reasons that will be examined later. The latest editor of the *News of the World*, David Montgomery, is the ninth since Rupert Murdoch first established a foothold in Fleet Street in 1968 by acquiring the paper from the Carr family in a series of adroit manoeuvres reminiscent of the prestidigitatious skills of the music hall performer who removes his victim's braces before his very eyes' with the aid of a disarming line in carefully constructed patter.

The character of the spectacular Murdoch coups which have added two of Britain's best-known qualities and its two biggest-selling down-market populars to a worldwide conglomerate embracing everything from newspapers to airlines, from radio and TV to a Hollywood film company, typifies the methods of the big business predators who have taken over most of Fleet Street. Although ownership of a paper is hardly a licence to print money in the TV tradition immortalised in the late Roy Thomson's *mot*, it is a licence to use the freedom of the press for the uninhibited exercise of personal licence if the proprietor chooses to exploit it – as some only too plainly do. The nature of their rise to power over the press, as much as their exercise of it, raises questions of national importance that a future government of the Left will have to tackle as a priority if access to the ownership of newspapers is to be regulated by qualifications more appropriate to democracy and a really free press than the size of a tycoon's chequebook.

Murdoch: The disappearing braces trick

It was predictive of the shape of things to come that when the first signs of the *News of the World's* financial troubles appeared in 1968 the two men who homed in on the stricken giant were Robert Maxwell and Rupert Murdoch, in that order, and that the battle for control that followed was marked by some of the most distasteful episodes in Fleet Street's not entirely tasteful history. The *News of the World* was still selling 6 million every Sunday with the prurient, titillating blend of detailed sex case reports and crime exposés that had earned it the trade sobriquet of 'Screws of the World', but profits had dropped sharply when Sir William Carr, head of the family that had controlled it for over 70 years, found a cousin was offering his 25 per cent block of shares to Maxwell, then a Labour MP and rising publisher who had long cherished the ambition to acquire his own newspaper. Alarmed at the prospect of a socialist – even a socialist entrepreneur – getting his hands on the paper, Carr, a dyed-in-the-wool Tory whose political views dominated its policy, began to look around for financial support while his editor, Stafford Somerfield, launched a deplorably chauvinistic attack on the Czech-born Maxwell that proclaimed the *NoW* was 'as British as roast beef . . . this is a British newspaper, run by British people. Let's keep it that way'. Maxwell, who had won the Military Cross in the British Army, was a naturalised citizen of the United Kingdom and had been a Member of Parliament for four years, was evidently not British enough to live on the immoral earnings of Britain's most salacious paper.

Murdoch, who had inherited two minor papers and by the age of 37 had carved himself a substantial sector of the Australian press and broadcasting media with a ruthlessness that had won him a reputation in a country where anything less in business is regarded as effete Pom-ism, was now finding his scope for further expansion cramped by the country's limited market. Already he had been planning an assault on Fleet Street, where he had done a brief apprentice stint on leaving Oxford, and was buying shares in the International Publishing Corporation. Alerted by merchant bankers Morgan Grenfell of the *NoW's* predicament, Murdoch flew immediately to London and moved in on the demoralised Carr to play his role as the shining white knight – not British, perhaps, but of British stock – who would save the roast beef of old Bouverie Street from the rapacious Czech dragon – for a modest reward. The initial deal was temptingly, and deceptively, simple: he would merge part of his £20m interests with the group's and add his rapidly bought-up stake in the *NoW* to the Carr family's 32 per cent to shut out Maxwell; in return he would become joint managing director, with Carr or one of his family remaining as chairman; and he agreed not to seek to increase his shareholding to secure absolute control. Then, as victory in the campaign for shareholder backing became clear, Murdoch modified the terms: he would become sole managing director, with Carr as chairman. Within three weeks, he was buying the disaffected cousin's shares. Three months later he asked Carr to resign as chairman and proposed himself for the job. By June 1969, eight months after his opening offer to protect Carr from the Czech menace, Rupert Murdoch was chairman and the *News of the World* was as British as kangaroo steak.

On to the next coup – *The Sun*

The *NoW* both whetted Murdoch's appetite for a bigger slice of the British national press and provided him with a ready-made plant for his next coup three months later in a second deal that reveals as much about the jungle ethics of Fleet Street as it does about Murdoch's methods. This time the paper was the *Sun*, which IPC was eager to shut down because of its £13m losses over eight years but was afraid to in case the print unions took out their anger on IPC's other papers, the two *Mirrors* and the *People*. For the *Sun* had special, if by now remote, tribal connotations for the trade union movement. In January 1961 when IPC's autocratic chairman, Cecil King, took over the huge Odhams magazine empire to shore up his group's shaky periodicals division, the ailing *Daily Herald*, founded in 1911 by printing workers and long the official paper of the unions and the Labour Party, and its Sunday sister the profitable *People*, a moderately leftish version of the *News of the World*, were part of the vast job lot. This huge takeover, adding two national papers to IPC's three, was the first big post-war step towards monopoly, but the Macmillan government rejected the outcry by Labour, the unions, sections of the press and the public, and refused to submit the deal to the Monopolies Commission. But the TUC still owned 49 per cent of the *Herald's* shares and King had to guarantee that he would keep the paper going for at least eight years.

After four years of mounting losses that earned it the label 'King's Cross', the *Herald* was transmogrified overnight into the *Sun*, 'the new paper born of the age we live in', designed by King's editorial henchman, Hugh (now Lord) Cudlipp, to a disastrous plastic formula based on extensive market research which had defined its potential readers as the 'steak-eating technocrats' of the era of white-hot technology promised by the new Labour prime minister, Harold Wilson. Neither of these phenomena was to materialise, so as soon as the eight-year guarantee was up, IPC decided to get rid of the albatross that Cudlipp, now chairman, believed was in fact a dying duck. Once again Maxwell, making much of his Labour connections, was first on the scene, but the editorial staff, unconvinced that he had the Messiah touch, blackballed his bid. Once again it was Murdoch who won the day, this time with a cheeky offer that Cudlipp was too desperate to refuse: £50,000 down and £250,000 over six years . . . if it lasted that long – and Cudlipp assumed that it wouldn't.

Having got Cudlipp over a barrel, Murdoch flatly rejected IPC's original stipulation – made in the interests of industrial relations rather than from any noble conviction – that the paper should keep faith with its Labour tradition. It was a bushranger's bargain in more senses than one. By warning the unions that unless they met his terms he would not begin to print, Murdoch was able to secure the most cost-effective manning agreement in Fleet Street: the editorial staff, for one, was less than half the size of the *Mirror's*. And the *NoW's* presses, idle six days a week, would now begin to earn their hitherto unprofitable keep.

There was no original journalistic magic in his dramatic transformation of Cudlipp's dying duck into the fatted goose that would lay the biggest golden egg in his News International group. Discerning the potentialities of the increasingly permissive 'swinging sixties', he simply translated the *News of the World's* traditional 'crumpet, crime and cricket' formula into daily terms and beefed it up in tabloid format with 'How to be a success in bed' features and the Page 3 naked nipples to attract the untapped sector of teenage comic-readers as well as the Andy Capp element of the *Mirror* readership, more interested in rape stories and racing tips that Cudlipp's admirable 'shock issues' on the wider problems of the human condition. Within a decade it was selling nearly four million and had overtaken the *Mirror*.

Murdoch says: 'I like to think of myself as a journalist.' He is, and a very able one of the raw, razmatazz school. But he is primarily a capitalist of the new brash Australian breed, an entrepreneur who happens by inheritance, like his contemporary Kerry Packer, to have started in what he always calls the communications industry; a restless predator with the killer instinct who revels in takeover battles, whether for newspapers or bauxite mines, as Michael Leapman relates in deadly detail in his biographical study, Barefaced Cheek. With his two British papers now bringing in money, Murdoch and his second wife Anna – still smarting from the Establishment snubs that followed the *News of the World's* heavily censured rehash of the Profumo-Keeler affair – emigrated once more, in 1973, this time to the United States, in search of new worlds to conquer, or at least take over. Two years and several American acquisitions later he was back in Britain in a bid to improve his image by buying the venerable but hard pressed *Observer*, whose increasing losses the Astor family could – or would – no longer underwrite. For once Murdoch was beaten at his own game by a backstairs ploy in which the paper and its deficit were transferred for a nominal price of £1 to an American oil company, Atlantic Richfield, with a public relations reputation for do-gooding that was to prove less than convincing, in the event (about which more later).

Revenge on the establishment

It was not until 1981 that Murdoch at last got his long-awaited chance to revenge himself on the Pom Establishment when a classic combination of union intransigence, crass managerial ineptitude and blatant political collusion delivered both *The Times* and the *Sunday Times* into his hands. For the whole of 1979 the two sister papers had been shut down by management lockout, at a loss of £40m, after a long dispute in which the neo-Luddite character of union resistance to the belated introduction of the 'new' technology – commonplace in the rest of the world – was well matched by the maladroit tactics and ill-judged bluster of the board, crowned by the impracticable terms of an ultimatum that merely provoked a disastrous showdown. By the time the papers were printing again the proprietor, Kenneth Thomson, who had inherited his father Roy's international chain in 1976 and moved its headquarters to Toronto, had had enough of the Fleet Street disease. A brief journalists' strike for 2 per cent more pay in August 1980 and projected losses of £13m for the year drove home the last nail: he decided to sell his father's pride and joy but, out of filial piety, only on terms that would include 'the interests of employees, readers and advertisers, the national interest as well as commercial and financial criteria'.

Inevitably, that well-known preoccupation of the national press, 'the national interest', ended up as an also-ran in the race for control that followed. The first-ever bid by journalists themselves to take over their papers and run them as co-operatives, financed by banks, City and even American money, got short shrift: one consortium was led by William Rees-Mogg, then editor of *The Times*, another by Harold Evans, editor of the *Sunday Times*, and a third organised by a staff group calling itself Journalists of The Times. 'Consortia cannot deal with unions,' decreed Gordon Brunton, Thomson's major domo in London and a key figure in the final deal. Some 40-odd big-money groups and alignments, ranging from the ubiquitous Maxwell and Rothermere's Associated Newspapers to Tiny Rowland, Atlantic Richfield, owners of the *Observer*, and Arab oil interests, got slightly longer shrift, but in what to many insiders looked like a fait accompli made in North America Murdoch emerged the winner. Incredibly, like the self-made millionaire who bought the golf club that had blackballed him, the man who had been attacked by *The Times* and *Sunday Times* for bringing journalism into disrepute had now got control of them both, for a mere £12m down and a solemn promise not to interfere with editorial decisions that provoked raucous hilarity among journalists from Sydney to New York. The disingenuousness of the Thomson Organisation's implicit argument that Murdoch was the only bidder who would be able, as an acknowledged strong-arm operator, to sort out the mess it had made of Times Newspapers and put the unions in their place, and therefore a protagonist of the public interest, was exceeded only by the cynicism explicit in the government's immediate approval of the takeover in what was clearly seen as its own political interest. From Mrs Thatcher's point of view, the proprietor of the *Sun* and the *News of the World*, who had stridently backed her in the 1979 election campaign, was eminently preferable politically, however deplorable his journalism, to all the alternative aspirants, with the possible exception of the equally right-wing Rothermere, owner of her favourite *Daily Mail*; the Mail yields to no Tory paper in its venomous approach to the Left in general and the Labour Party and trade unions in particular, but its circulation is barely 2 million compared with the combined 8 million of Murdoch's two tabloids.

Turning a Nelsonian eye to the principle of the Fair Trading Act, which stipulates that the sale of a viable newspaper should be referred to the Monopolies Commission, the then Secretary of State for Trade, John Biffen, approved the merger within three days of the sale in January 1981. Despite the evidence that the *Sunday Times* had long been profitable as an entity within the Times Newspapers group and was calculated to increase its profits to £13m within three years, Biffen ruled that 'neither *The Times* nor *Sunday Times* is economic as a going concern and as a separate newspaper' and argued that as Thomson intended to close them that month unless a deal was reached this made impractical any referral to the Monopolies Commission, which would not be able to report within two months. Biffen's statement of consent contained eight conditions 'guaranteeing' the independence of the two editors and stipulating that they 'shall not be appointed or dismissed without the approval of the majority of the independent national directors', appointed earlier as watchdogs. Hand on heart, Murdoch told the staff of *The Times*: 'What if I found a way of tearing up all those guarantees and fired an editor? The answer is there would be a terrible public stink and it would destroy the paper'. Exactly a year later his personal choice as editor of *The Times*, Harold Evans, whom he had hailed as 'the greatest editor in the world', had been given the disappearing braces treatment in a calculated performance watched not only by the six independent but bemused national directors* and Mr Biffen, in his role as Pilate, but the public at large as *The Times* reported the progress of the putsch, with deadpan objectivity, and the broadcasters haunted Gray's Inn Road for quotes from the two factions what were forming under Evans and his deputy, Charles Douglas-Home, active Murdoch supporter and his choice for the chair when Evans was ousted.

The safeguards that weren't

As Evans reveals in his book, *Good Times, Bad Times*, Murdoch was too practised in the art of sacking editors to resort simply to tearing up the guarantees – he merely stepped up the pressure for his resignation until the 'atmosphere of intrigue, fear and spite' finally forced him to quit in despair without formally calling on the independent directors to intervene. Whether Murdoch wanted to be rid of Evans largely because of his refusal to move *The Times* further to the Right in support of the Thatcher-Reagan axis, as Evans declares, or because of the undoubted deep divisions he had generated among the editorial staff by his methods and the introduction of his own senior executives, or for a combination of

---

* The six national directors of Times Newspapers in 1981 were: Lord Robens, former Labour minister turned businessman; Lord Dacre, the historian Hugh Trevor-Roper; Lord (Sid) Greene, former secretary of the National Union of Railwaymen; Lord Roll, merchant banker and former civil servant; Sir Denis Hamilton, editor-in-chief, Times Newspapers, until the takeover; Sir Edward Pickering, former chairman of IPC and ex-editor of Beaverbrook's *Daily Express*.

both, one thing is clear: Murdoch had both exposed the hollowness of the government's pretence that Biffen's safeguards would guarantee the independence of his editors and had at the same time delighted Mrs Thatcher by giving both papers an explicit Tory line.

Murdoch's publicly expressed contempt for the 'all-pervasive elitism' of British society and the relative wetness of even Mrs Thatcher herself underlies his cavalier attitude to the terms of the Times Newspapers takeover. Although Biffen's second condition laid down that 'future disposals are to be subject to the consent of a majority of the independent national directors', he removed the titles of both papers from the ownership of Times Newspapers and vested them in News International, without consulting them, only ten months after the takeover. This meant that in the event of his decision to liquidate TNL (which he had threatened during a union stoppage) no other publisher would have been able to revive the titles. For once he was thwarted: Rees-Mogg (now Sir William), who as editor had given the takeover his blessing, pointed out to Biffen that the transfer was unlawful. Murdoch quickly revoked the title switch. But his determination to secure total domination of his four British national papers was demonstrated in 1983 when he bought out the last remaining publicly held shares in News International, his British company, to bring it under full control of the Australian-based parent group.

Although the hoary old cliché still creeps into the headlines, *The Times* has not been 'The Thunderer' since the days of the great Delane. What reputation it had left after its years under Northcliffe never really recovered from its pre-war policy of the Thirties when the editor, Geoffrey Dawson, spiked the truth about Hitler. Yet at worst it is one of the tiny minority of serious British newspapers. It is a grim comment on the nature of the free enterprise which governs Fleet Street that it should have ended up as just another entry in the books of an international entrepreneur who could be said to have made a fortune out of the unacceptable face of journalism. It is an even grimmer comment on the state of Britain that earlier this year the nation could watch on television as the Queen marked the 200th anniversary of *The Times* by graciously sharing a joke with the man whose *Sun*, just two years before, was taken to court in the Palace's first-ever legal action to protect the royal family's privacy and made to pay £4,000 to charity for its 'revelations' about the relationship between Prince Andrew and his actress friend Koo Stark. For those who care about the role of newspapers in our kind of democracy, Rupert Murdoch is no laughing matter. A man who is prepared to change his nationality to secure control of an American TV network means business – at almost any price.

Rowland: Behind the editor's back

Although he may have proved to be less skilled in the techniques of ousting editors, Tiny Rowland, chairman of Lonrho, who gained control of the *Observer* in 1981, a month after Rupert Murdoch's capture of Times Newspapers, has a reputation for ruthlessness in his business dealings that rivals, if not exceeds, the Australian's: a Department of Trade report in the 1970s criticising his company's controversial activities and questioning his commercial ethics evoked from the then prime minister, Edward Heath, the memorable condemnation of Lonrho as 'the unpleasant and unacceptable face of capitalism'. The damning label was given the full treatment by the press but it proved to be no drawback when he joined the millionaire newspaper proprietors' club in a secret deal that shook even the hardened El Vino cynics of Fleet Street. Rowland, born in India in 1917 of a German father named Furhop and an English mother, had farmed in Rhodesia after the war before his meteoric, and controversial, rise to the top of the Lonrho empire.

The *Observer*, founded in 1791, only six years after *The Times*, had won an enviable reputation for the quality of its liberal journalism and particularly its Third World coverage under the enlightened post-war editorship of David Astor, a member of the family trust that owned it, but eroding circulation and a plague of damaging stoppages to secure union pay demands brought heavy losses. In 1976 Astor looked round for a buyer who would maintain the paper's high standards and tradition of editorial independence. Predictably, the familiar stage army of would-be owners, headed by Murdoch, Maxwell, Sir James Goldsmith, and Rothermere, lined up with their offers, joined by several Arab oil interests, a Libyan government nominee, Olga Deterding, a British heiress, and Sally Aw Sian, a Hong Kong publisher, among numerous others. The chances of finding the right proprietor to maintain the *Observer's* standards seemed bleak when a chance meeting between Kenneth Harris, one of its senior writers, and an American friend, Professor Douglas Cater, resulted in an offer by Robert O. Anderson, chairman of Atlantic Richfield, a Los Angeles oil company, which promised to save the paper from a fate worse than death and guarantee a secure future. Arco would take a 90 per cent interest and the Observer Trust, headed by the ubiquitous Lord Goodman, would retain 10 per cent.

In a euphoric three-page fanfare the *Observer* hailed Anderson as a business leader with a strong social conscience whose firm's foundation had donated millions to medical and cultural causes. On Page 1 Anderson himself declared: 'I believe the *Observer's* future can be as long and illustrious as its past ... we see no reason to believe that it cannot continue as a strong and viable publication'. *The Times*, still owned then by the Thomson organisation (which itself has large North Sea oil interests) reported pointedly that by saving the *Observer* ARCO might improve its chances of getting Department of Energy approval for its current application for offshore oil exploration licences. But the machine managers' chapel of the National Graphical Association had also smelt the sweet scent of oil money and a long series of costly stoppages began. Defying the union's national leadership, the chapel repeatedly kept the paper off the news-stands to back its demands for more staff, more pay and its objections to the introduction of new technology. By 1980 ARCO, with losses of £8m, was running out of patience, although not out of cash – the group's revenue for the year was forecast to top £6,000m.

On 25 February 1981, only five years into the 'long and illustrious future', Atlantic Richfield ended its ownership abruptly in a secret deal behind the paper's back that smacked more of low practice than high-minded stewardship. Anderson had been in London for a board meeting and the board had baulked at his surprise proposal to make Kenneth Harris, the original go-between, vice-chairman over the editor's head. All seemed well, however, when he took off again for America. Then came a telephone call from Los Angeles that rocked the paper: without reference to the board, the editor or the Trade Secretary, Anderson had handed over control of the paper to Tiny Rowland, whose public reputation had still not recovered from Heath's scathing denunciation. The financial deal was clear-cut: ARCO were to exchange the *Observer* for a 40 per cent stake in Outram, Lonrho's Scottish newspaper group, worth some £6m, and Anderson would remain chairman. For Rowland the dividends would be potentially twofold: control of a newspaper noted for its coverage and influential views on affairs in Africa, where Lonrho made much of its profits, and a facelift for his image in his new role as saviour of 'one of the world's great newspapers'.

The feckless amateur watchdogs

In an angry letter to *The Times* (itself still in the throes of the Murdoch takeover) David Astor condemned the secret deal, pointed out prophetically that as a result 'the number of countries where the *Observer* would have to be editorially careful would be great' and demanded that the government refer the matter to the Monopolies Commission. Anderson and Rowland immediately altered the terms of their arrangement to obviate such an investigation, but the growing storm of criticism forced the government's hand. Predictably, Biffen approved the takeover with the now familiar condition that five independent directors be appointed to protect the editor's freedom – but only after Donald Trelford, the editor, with characteristic vigour, had lambasted the Commission for its naive and feckless amateurism. In a damning exposé of its methods after the event, Trelford revealed that it admitted it had not intended to call him to give evidence although it had sought the views of the Institute of Journalists, the smaller of the two journalists' unions, none of whose members were employed by the *Observer*; but, it had agreed, he was welcome to do so 'like any other member of the public'. The Commission's procedures, declared Trelford, make it incapable of producing a recommendation which takes account of 'the need for accurate presentation of news and free expression of opinion' as required in newspaper mergers by Section 59 of the Fair Trading Act. The Monopolies Commission, he said, was 'dangerously misinformed about the way newspapers actually work, especially the role of the editor and the complex relationship between editorial and management'. He also pointed out that the Commission had no practical idea how the five national directors were supposed to safeguard his independence although their appointment was specifically intended to remove any threat to complete freedom of expression. Trelford concluded that the *Observer* owed its continuing editorial independence to the 'lucky coincidence that Murdoch had agreed, only months before, on similar editorial guarantees at Times Newspapers – ironically, to avoid a reference to the Commission. Since the Secretary for Trade had given his public blessing to those guarantees he could hardly agree that the *Observer* be sold with fewer or less solid guarantees'.

Those guarantees were soon to be tested. In 1983, without consulting Trelford, Rowland appointed Godwin Matatu, a Zimbabwean political 'fixer' employed by Lonrho to smooth relations between Rowland and Prime Minister Mugabe, as an accredited roving correspondent in Africa for the *Observer*, but paid by Lonrho. The foreign editor resigned and the editorial staff blacked Matatu's copy, but Trelford eventually worked out a compromise that avoided a full-scale showdown. That was to come six months later. In April 1984 Trelford flew to Harare to interview Mugabe on the fourth anniversary of Zimbabwe's independence, the day after Rowland himself had had a lengthy meeting with the prime minister. While there Trelford also took the opportunity of visiting Matabeleland, home of Joshua Nkomo's Zapu party resistance to Mugabe's rule and banned to foreign journalists. When he got back to London, Trelford published, not the formal interview with Mugabe which Rowland had enthusiastically urged, but a grim full-page account of the campaign of widespread killing and brutality waged by Mugabe's notorious Fifth Brigade. Infuriated by this demonstration of editorial independence, Rowland wrote a letter of abject apology to Mugabe in which he attacked Trelford as 'discourteous, disingenuous and wrong' for publishing 'a sensational article based on unsubstantiated, unresearched material'. In an unparallelled public slanging match that followed Rowland declared that he had three alternatives: to close down the paper, to sell it ('and nobody's going to tell me whom I shall sell it to') or to sack Trelford. To underline his threat, he withdrew all Lonrho advertising from the paper, worth some £20,000 a week, and announced that he would be prepared to sell the *Observer* to Robert Maxwell, waiting as ever in the wings, if the price were right.

It was at this point that the five independent directors acted. At *The Times* its equivalent watchdogs had been left sitting on the sidelines looking on like Murdoch's poodles because Harold Evans, with his staff split down the middle, felt that there was no point in calling on the directors' help to curb Murdoch's campaign to unseat him. At the *Observer* the journalists, unanimously behind Trelford, demanded a meeting with the directors, who proved to be made of sterner mettle. After talking with both sides, the guardians of the 190-year-old paper's ark of independence rebuked Rowland for 'improper interference with the editorial freedom of the newspaper'. They had also been at work behind the scenes to patch up the damage and bring owner and editor together in a truce, however uneasy. Trelford wrote to Rowland, offering to resign if that was the price of Lonrho's continued financial support for the paper but also proffering an olive branch *pour encourager*: 'I accept that you acted as you did, not out of a crude concern for your commercial interests, as I originally suggested, but out of a genuine personal conviction that the truth about Zimbabwe is more complex than I presented it'. In a breathtaking volte face, Rowland replied: 'I support your editorship and I refuse to accept your resignation ... it seems to me an absolute demonstration of your integrity and care for the paper that, although there is no need for you to offer your resignation, you have done so'.

To complete the rapprochement, Rowland promised increased investment in the paper 'until the *Observer* is No 1 in the field'. This sudden access of goodwill was not extended to the independent directors who had had the temerity to exercise their statutory independence. Dismissing the five distinguished public figures* as 'troglodytes', and threatening to cut their annual emoluments, Rowland declared: 'I can't see that they have any future role to play.' The truth is, of course, that the directors, particularly the late William Clark, stymied his bid to do a Murdoch: as a later chapter will suggest, independent arbiters of such calibre, armed with appropriate powers, could have a vital transitional role to play in the democratisation of the control of all newspapers, the populars as well as the qualities.

Maxwell: The price of a sell-out

It could be argued that if ever a man needed his own newspaper it was Robert Maxwell. Throughout his meteoric, chequered and much-headlined career he has had a worse press than even Sir James Goldsmith. And the 'bouncing Czech', as Fleet Street gleefully punned from the time that doubts about his financial techniques and marketing methods first surfaced in the City pages in the late Sixties, was determined from his earliest days to own at least one, no matter how many rebuffs, no matter how long it took. In the 15 years from his *News of the World* defeat at the hands of Murdoch until he finally landed the Mirror group in July 1984 no newspaper deal had taken place without a bid from Maxwell. Most of them never reached the short list, not least because of the smell that still lingered, faint but persistent, from his official branding as a questionable operator, despite the deodorising effect of his Phoenix-like comeback from the ashes of a City scandal of the early Seventies. But Reed International's nostrils proved to be more robust than the sense of honour that initially had inspired its commendable pledge to keep the hands of predatory tycoons off the last of the Labour-supporting national papers.

Maxwell, like Murdoch, Rowland and Matthews, is one of the post-war genus of millionaires who have acquired their financial power, and *ergo* their newspapers, by manipulating rather than making like the old-fashioned industrialists. For them the takeover of other people's creations has been the short-cut to the top, buying out control from established firms, ruthlessly rejigging them to maximise profit or stripping their assets to raise the price of the next purchase. Maxwell is well equipped with the qualities essential for this brand of free enterprise freebooting: outstanding business acumen, boundless energy, risk-courage (with an MC to prove it), overweening ambition, calculated ruthlessness, an insatiable appetite for money-power and its conspicuous symbols, and unlimited reserves of *chutzpah*.

* The independent directors appointed to the *Observer* board were: Sir Derek Mitchell, former Treasury civil servant, senior adviser to Lehman Brothers, investment bankers; William Clark, ex-Vice President of the World Bank and former *Observer* writer; Sir Geoffrey Cox, co-founder of Independent Television News and former political correspondent of the *News Chronicle*; Dame Rosemary Murray, former Vice-Chancellor of Cambridge University; Lord Windlesham, former managing director of Associated Television.

Having exchanged his birth names, Jan Ludvik Koch, for a sonorous Scottish set, Ian Robert Maxwell, and acquired a perfect command of unaccented English in the British Army, from which he had just been demobilised, the gallant young ex-Czech ex-officer started up in the publishing business with some high quality printing plates he had acquired, with typical foresight, in Germany, where he had ended up as head of the Foreign Office press section, a job that aroused an interest in newspapers that was to become a ruling passion. In 1949 he bought the old-established Pergamon Press for £13,000 and took off. By 1964 Pergamon was reputedly the world's biggest scientific and educational publisher and Maxwell was Labour MP for Buckingham with a finger in every pie that offered either profit or prestige, from computer technology to the Council of Europe, headlined all the way.

Six years later his spectacular rocket was on its way back down to earth. He lost his seat in the 1970 election, was severely criticised for his handling of constituency affairs and his political career disappeared under a local cloud. An even bigger cloud was looming on the business horizon. The Department of Trade began to investigate Pergamon after an involved but unsuccessful attempt to merge it with an American computer firm named Leasco. Maxwell, concluded the Department's inspectors, was 'not a person who can be relied upon to exercise proper stewardship of a publicly quoted company'. He was now *persona non grata* in the City where prejudice coloured the criticism. What might have shattered the confidence of a thinner-skinned type merely proved to be a further challenge to Maxwell's resilience. In 1974, undeterred by his fall from Harold Wilson's favour, he again contested Buckingham, although he failed to win back the seat. More significantly, however, he won back the chair at Pergamon and took off on his second business career, brushing aside the Trade Department's report as a temporary and unfair irrelevance. By 1980 he had secured control of the giant but struggling British Printing Corporation and turned a £6.7m loss into a £5m profit in a year, cutting thousands of jobs in a massive reconstruction programme of closures and mergers that provoked a showdown with the printing unions. It was a bitter battle but Maxwell won on points. At last he was really in the big league, eagerly on the lookout once more for the paper he yearned to own and mastermind.

Beaten to the draw once more

Yet again, however, he was thwarted, in 1981, as Murdoch hijacked *The Times* and Rowland pulled off his backstairs coup at the

Observer. Even when Reed International revealed in October 1983 that it planned to sell Mirror Group Newspapers – the *Daily Mirror*, *Sunday Mirror*, *Sunday People*, *Sporting Life* and two Scottish titles, the *Daily Record* and *Sunday Mail* – Maxwell's way into Fleet Street seemed blocked once more. Reed's chairman, Sir Alex Jarratt, announced that to safeguard the papers' 'traditions and character and editorial independence' the share capital would be distributed among a large number of ordinary shareholders to keep predators at bay: no single offer from an individual or organisation would be entertained and an independent chairman with Labour sympathies but also acceptable to City institutions would be appointed. The surprise choice for what promised to be a very hot seat was Clive Thornton, a deceptively modest-looking solicitor of impeccable working-class origins who had shaken up the building society movement as head of Abbey National. Once again a bid by journalists to take over and run their own newspapers failed when Reed turned down an offer of £100m from a consortium of MGN editorial staffs backed by two merchant banks. The reason, explained Reed, was that it was determined that the papers should not fall under the control of any one group or faction, even its journalists.

This admirable policy, on the face of it, reflected Reed's high-minded sense of duty towards the two *Mirrors'* (now much dissipated) radical heritage. *The Mirror*, founded by Northcliffe as a gentlewomen's chatty daily in 1903, had by the Thirties become a company owned by general shareholders and masterminded by a rough diamond Cockney, Harry Guy Bartholomew, who built up a mass circulation with an inspired formula combining 'light' human interest features, brilliant projection of hard news, decorous pin-ups, Jane and other comic strips, and a strong populist-socialist line that played a seminal part in Labour's 1945 victory. But six years later 'Bart' had been ousted in a putsch led by Cecil King, Northcliffe's nephew, who shared his uncle's Napoleonic tendencies and proceeded to turn his renamed International Publishing Corporation into the biggest publishing group in the world, taking over newspapers and magazines until, in 1965, it owned 230 titles and employed 30,000 people.

But if the original steak-eaters' *Sun* had been IPC's albatross Reed was certainly its cuckoo. As the autocratic King was building his mammoth but ramshackle empire in the Sixties he bought a 28 per cent slice of Reed Paper with an eye to newsprint supplies. But in 1968 King, now firmly in the grip of Northcliffean *folie de grandeur*, cleared the Mirror's front page for an imperial personal article demanding Harold Wilson's resignation as prime minister and was himself promptly putsched. As the dust cleared it was revealed that

King's far-flung empire was in a financial and structural mess. In the merger with Reed to streamline the set-up IPC found itself to be only one of ten divisions in a reorganised conglomerate ranging from wallpaper and packaging to paint and DIY. Officially, MGN retained full editorial independence under Hugh Cudlipp, chairman of IPC, but the Mirror's old verve and nerve deserted it as Murdoch's soft-porn *Sun* began to overtake it. Fatally, it began to copy what Cudlipp had once dismissed as a "poor carbon copy" of the *Mirror*. As sales fell – from 5 million in the Sixties to under $3\frac{1}{2}$ million in 1981 – and MGN lost £3.2m on revenue of £125m, Jarratt sought a way to get rid of the embarrassing incubus. He made no secret of his admiration for Mrs Thatcher's policies (he had known her in his days as a civil servant) or of his distaste for the Mirror's editorial views but insisted that he did not interfere with its politics. It is noteworthy, however, that in the 1983 election the *Mirror* achieved a remarkable feat of intellectual contortion by urging readers to vote Labour while declaring that it was totally opposed to Labour's central policies of withdrawal from the EEC, unilateral nuclear disarmament and rejection of all pay controls. But this flight of political schizophrenia wasn't enough to dissuade Jarratt, wrestling with Reed's wider problems. With the election over and Mrs Thatcher back in Downing Street, the Reed chairman at last found the long-sought *deus ex machina* in the shape of Reuters. The famous international news agency had quietly turned into a spectacular money-spinner since the Sixties, not by its traditional function of supplying overseas copy to the newspapers which collectively owned it but by establishing a global network that provided a 24-hour service of instant business information and market intelligence to some 35,000 subscribers throughout the commercial world. Profits had risen by 400 per cent, it was planning to go public in 1984 and Reed's share looked as if it could be worth anything from £75m upwards – enough to provide a sweetener for potential shareholders when MGN went to the market at a proposed figure of £100m-plus.

Head of the queue at last

The papers' new chairman, Clive Thornton, announced that readers and staff would be offered the chance to buy 'Mirror bonds' at £50-100 as part of the plan to spread the share capital as widely as possible. 'One thing is absolutely certain,' he said, 'no one person will be able to buy it up.' He should have known that the only absolutely certain thing in the City is its endemic uncertainty. In February 1984 the City institutions turned down Thornton's scheme to create a multiple-share structure as a takeover-blocking device. Plainly editorial independence was not a marketable commodity. And after a similar City row about its own takeover-blocking plans the Reuters flotation proved to be less than the much-hyped bonanza, coming as it did during a sudden collapse in London share prices. MGN profits had slumped to £¼m, the market was unpromising, the sweetener was turning sour – the *Mirror* and its sister papers were now up for grabs.

At long last Maxwell found himself to his unconcealed delight to be at the head of, indeed the only member of, the queue. On 3 July 1984 he offered Reed £80m but his bid was turned down, however reluctantly. Fearing the storm of protest such a deal would provoke from Labour and the print unions, Jarratt insisted publicly that the board would abide by its pledge to sell to the public at large. No one knows the price of a pledge better than Maxwell. He immediately raised the ante to £113.4m and publicly played the card he knew would count with the Reed board, looking over their shoulders at their shareholders: 'I cannot see', he said, 'how it can justify turning down more cash on the table than it would receive through the market place' (estimated at about £60m). To clinch his offer he promised to maintain the papers' political line and editorial policies. But Jarratt assured Thornton on 10 July that there would be no sale to a single buyer. Just before midnight on 12 July Jarratt accepted Maxwell's cheque: that extra £33m had seen off the last of Reed's scruples.

When Clive Thornton arrived at the *Mirror* office next morning he found Maxwell already installed at his desk and his dreams of a democratic managerial-editorial co-operative in the wastepaper basket. 'I am the proprietor, 100 per cent,' Maxwell proclaimed to the assembled fathers of the papers' myriad chapels, 'and I want that to be understood very clearly. There can only be one boss and that's me!' Sir Alex Jarratt, like the good civil servant he used to be, summed up the sell-out in Whitehall-type euphemisms: 'The board had to weigh their announced strategic objective of disposing of MGN as well as the very large disparity between Pergamon's final offer and the likely final outcome of the available alternatives. I have no doubt that the board's decision was correct and in the best interests of Reed International's shareholders.' An ebullient Maxwell put the deal in sharper perspective: 'The cash in MGN, its shareholding in Reuters and the buildings together are equal to what I paid for it. The papers are in for free.' Editors would be allowed to produce their papers 'without interference with their editorial judgment and freedom' but 'they must and will have a Britain-first policy' and they would 'fight for the return of a Labour government at the next election'. Swallowing Maxwell's coup and braggadocio with obvious difficulty, Neil Kinnock, leader of the Labour Party, welcomed the unwelcome takeover with a cautious use of the conditional mood: 'The history of single-proprietor ownership of newspapers in Britain is not a happy one. Mr Maxwell could be the exception to the rule. Many people will join me in hoping that he will be.'

Back on the takeover trail

Such hopes were to be shorter-lived than Clive Thornton's brief stay in the chairman's office as Maxwell quickly imposed his gauche and all-pervasive narcissism on the group in general and the *Mirror* in particular, filling it with pictures of himself and his numerous family and Barnum publicity stunts in which he inevitably played the starring role: flying the *Mirror's* own food plane to starving Ethiopia, careering round Britain in the *Mirror's* own train with an entourage of embarrassed, not to say humiliated, editors and senior journalists, to find out 'What the readers really want', presenting a cheque for £1m to Maudie, the winner of his 'new, bigger and better' bingo competition, designed to upstage the *Sun* by creating the first reader-millionaire (Murdoch once again outsmarted him by organising his £1m winner first).

But Maxwell was not too busy adding this new personalised dimension to junk journalism to neglect any opportunity to add another to his string of companies. Three months after his *Mirror* victory he made a bid for Britain's largest cable-TV network, but ran into a legal snag – the Cable and Broadcasting Act does not allow British cable operations to be controlled from outside the EEC, to which Liechtenstein does not belong, and the tiny tax-haven statelet is where Pergamon Holding Foundation, master body of the conglomerate, is based. To get round this little difficulty, Maxwell set up a personal British-based company and the deal went through before Christmas. Meanwhile, through BPCC, he had renewed his long-running battle for control of John Waddington, a printing and packaging firm best known for its ownership of the Monopoly board game. Waddington rejected and eventually beat off his £44m bid on several grounds but the one that made the headlines – except in *Mirror* Group papers – was inspired by none other than Clive Thornton, citing a law under which a refusal to reveal the ultimate beneficial ownership of a company could lead to the disfranchising of shares. 'It is of fundamental importance that we should know who ultimately controls BPCC,' said Waddington. It was a question the rest of the press eagerly sought an answer to, but Maxwell, angrily denouncing such investigative journalism as a 'witch-hunt', denied categorically that he owns or controls the Pergamon Holding Foundation. The man who had boasted 'I am the proprietor, 100 per cent' when he marched into the *Mirror* now said that he had always described himself as the publisher and no more.

Who then controls *Mirror* Group Newspapers and the rest of what the world had long believed to be Maxwell's empire? 'Sources close to Mr Maxwell,' reported the Australian-owned *Times* of London, 'have confirmed that the foundation owners are Mrs Maxwell's family interests in France.' The *Mirror*, proud standard bearer of Maxwell's 'Britain-first policy', is, it seems, as British as *boeuf bourguignon*.

Matthews: Exit four editors, enter bingo

When Victor (now Lord) Matthews emerged through the tradesmen's entrance, as it were, to take over the *Daily Express* group in 1977 he could boast two qualifications that marked him out from the other three entrepreneurs stalking Fleet Street in the continuing hunt for a personal newspaper, even if his main qualification was the usual corporate chequebook: he was British born (Islington) and he came of working-class stock. But any hope that he might prove to be a second 'Bart', bringing back the dynamic radicalism and earthy flair with which his fellow Cockney had once invigorated the *Mirror* and balanced the political coloration of the national newspaper scene, was quickly dispelled. Like so many who have come up the hard way to success in business, Matthews had become a no-nonsense boss and ardent Tory with a Tebbiteseque view of those who haven't had the gumption to pull themselves up to the boardroom by their own bootstraps. The late Lord Beaverbrook might be revolving in the Happy Hunting Grounds of the New Brunswick sky like a Shoe Lane press in mid-edition, at the sight of his beloved papers being knocked down to a builder in one of Fleet Street's more byzantine auctions, but at least the *Express* brand of jingo-patriotism and its 'You, too, can be a millionaire' approach to the redistribution of wealth were in safe hands.

Matthews's first contact with the *Express* was as a building worker for Trollope & Colls, which had been Beaverbrook's construction contractors for half a century. The boy who left school at 14 and joined the firm after war service proved to be a brilliant manager and had risen to deputy chairman and managing director of Trafalgar

House, Nigel Broackes's conglomerate, which had expanded from property into building and shipping, taking over Trollope on the way, by the early seventies when Sir Max Aitken called in the firm to redevelop the Beaverbrook site. The *Express* and *Evening Standard* were physically integrated, new presses installed, preparations made for the eventual introduction of the new technology and a new office block built on the Standard site to produce some much-needed income. But the costly new plant did nothing to stop the circulation rot that had set in even before the death in 1964 of Beaverbrook, the malevolent genius who had made the *Express* the synonym for Fleet Street success. So when the ailing Sir Max decided in 1976 to sell his equally ailing inheritance no one was better placed to cash in, literally, on his inside information than Vic Matthews. He offered Trafalgar's help and waited. But in the familiar Fleet Street tradition – as Lewis Chester and Jonathan Fenby revealed in their *The Fall of the House of Beaverbrook*, an example to all would-be investigative journalists – Sir Max was already dickering secretly with Vere Harmsworth (later to succeed to the Rothermere title), head of Associated Newspapers, owners of the *Daily Mail*, the *Express*'s hereditary rival and itself losing money, like its sister paper the *Evening News*.

Next on the scene was Rupert Murdoch, who offered to put £10m into Beaverbrook Newspapers on condition that he could bring in his own management team to get the group back into profit, of which he would want a percentage. This uncharacteristically disinterested offer, ostensibly to extend and strengthen Murdoch's efforts to tame the print unions, would not merely have unseated both Jocelyn Stevens, the chief executive, and Charles Wintour, now managing director of the *Express*, but could provide an ideal stage for the Australian's disappearing braces act. Meanwhile Sir James Goldsmith, the dynamic and controversial young (43) international entrepreneur, inveterate critic of the press and long-time seeker after a foothold in Fleet Street, revealed that he had bought a third of Beaverbrook non-voting stock and proposed that he should therefore join the board. Once again he got the brush-off. Goldsmith – newly knighted by the Wilson government – is not easily kept at bay: he now teamed up with his fellow tycoon Tiny Rowland for a joint bid. To underline his suitability for the responsibilities of newspaper ownership, Goldsmith, a prolific initiator of libel writs, ended his much-criticised action against *Private Eye* for criminal libel after an agreed public apology from its editor, Richard Ingrams, orchestrated by Stevens, Wintour and Simon Jenkins, his protégé and successor as editor of the Standard. This instant whitewash, however, was to prove of no avail.

Trafalgar's £12½ million trump card

Behind the scenes Harmsworth was building up Associated's stake in Beaverbrook for another go, encouraged by seemingly approving signals from Sir Max. It was then Matthews played Trafalgar's trump card. Every other option involved either the possibility, however remote, of a Monopolies Commission veto, the merging or disappearance of titles, not to mention senior management, or opposition from both journalists and production unions. Trafalgar's offer was disarmingly clear cut: £12½m for the shares, a pledge to keep all three titles alive – subject to profitability, of course – no major boardroom changes and no compulsory redundancies. It all seemed to be too good to be true, as indeed it turned out to be. But it was an offer Sir Max and his family foundation could hardly refuse if they were to get out from under with the minimum amount of blood on the carpet. The self-made man from the building site whose main reading until then had been the racing pages of the *Daily Express* was now its boss, announcing with all the gravitas of a Samuel Goldwyn that his editors would have a completely free hand as long as they kept to his policies. His other pronouncements as he addressed the media in his syntactically unsophisticated style, flushed with an intoxicating new kind of power, betrayed not merely his unfamiliarity with the dramatis personae and terminology of the newspaper scene but a disconcerting ignorance of the complex and archaic nature of the Fleet Street brontosaurus.

Matthews had acquired a reputation as Nigel Broackes's strong right arm in Trafalgar's dealings with the assorted workforces it had taken over and taken on, but he was to meet his match in the *Express* chapels. 'A lot of troubles in Fleet Street are due to weak management,' he said patronisingly, if truthfully, after winning a court ruling that Sogat must not curtail production of extra copies of the *Express* – and therefore prevent Matthews from cashing in – while the *Mirror* was shut down by a journalists' dispute. His prediction that this was the beginning of the end of union power in Fleet Street was to prove that his naivety was not restricted to semantics; it also underlined the complete lack of solidarity among members of the Newspaper Publishers' Association which had laid the foundations for the growth of union power he was now trying to challenge.

If a pluralist press were desirable as an end in itself, Matthews would have to be congratulated on having added another title to the list of national newspapers (he had already been party to the subtraction of one title from Fleet Street by merging the *Standard* with Rothermere's *Evening News* in a joint-ownership deal in 1980). His reasons for inventing the *Daily Star* in 1978 and its subsequent contribution to junk journalism do little, however, for the theory that more newspapers can only be good for democracy. After a series of confrontations in his first few months that taught him any negotiations with UCATT and the National Union of Seamen had been love feasts in comparison with the bargaining tactics of newspaper chapels in pursuit of what he called 'monstrous pay claims' – such as stopping production for several days and allegedly sabotaging machinery – Matthews threatened to move the whole *Express* operation to Manchester. The unions, knowing that the *Express* is not the QE2, called his bluff.

But the idea of Manchester, with its relatively moderate and moderately paid workforce, stuck in Matthews's mind. If the London chapels would not give up their overmanned featherbed he would split *Express* overheads by producing another paper at the Manchester plant and challenge the *Sun*, which prints only in London. A year later the *Star* appeared, indistinguishable in formula from the *Sun* except for the masthead, the fact that its daily ration of naked nipples appeared on Page 7 instead of Page 3, and a noticeably more open-minded attitude to Labour and the unions than the *Express* from which it had been cloned – a policy conceived with entrepreneurial cynicism to seduce the less intellectual strata of the *Mirror* readership in the then still Labour-voting conurbations north of Watford rather than in the spirit of C P Scott's dictum about editorial fairness. In the event not even its introduction of bingo, Matthews's most notable contribution to newspaper development so far has been able to raise the *Star*'s sales – now 1.4 million – above the loss-making level. Five editors later the *Express* has slumped to 1.8 million and the *Sunday* – one editor since 1954 – has shed 2 million since its peak sales in the 1960s and is still slipping.

Floating off to independence

It would be unfair, however, not to point out that at least he freed *Express* Newspapers from its uneasy position as a mere adjunct of the flourishing Trafalgar conglomerate, with all that such vassal status implies for real press freedom, when he risked the demerging of the newspapers and the Morgan Grampian magazine group from Trafalgar as a separate company under the Fleet Holdings title. At least the papers are now part of an independent publishing group, although Fleet owes its discrete identity less to Matthews's desire for independence than to Broackes's wish to end an embarrassing commercial relationship. 'There is an irritation that reflects on

Trafalgar,' he told the shareholders, 'if some social or gossip item appears in the paper . . . it has been a fair irritant on the board.' Even more irritating, Matthews revealed in his refreshingly unbuttoned way, was that because Trollope & Coll had become a sister company of the *Express* other newspaper proprietors no longer placed their lucrative development contracts with it.

Fleet Holdings has been a moderate financial success, with pre-tax profits doubled to £11m in 1984 and the revenue from its £80m stake in Reuters. But already United Newspapers, owners of the third largest chain of provincial newspapers (40), including the strongly Tory *Yorkshire Post*, *Punch* and other magazines as well as large American interests, and headed by David Stevens, a youngish banker with ambitions to join the new press baronage, has acquired 20 per cent of Fleet (most of it bought from the ubiquitous Maxwell) for a takeover bid that is being mounted at the moment of writing after being given the go-ahead by the Department of Trade. Whatever happens, Matthews will have become an even richer millionaire: he received £1.6m for his Trafalgar shares and stands to make even more from his large Fleet holding. More important from the point of view of the public interest, if United Newspapers win control of Fleet it will form another huge new media group and intensify the concentration of press ownership in fewer hands.

The floating off of Fleet highlights the paradox that militates against the emergence of a diverse national press under present conditions: the price of a newspaper's economic independence is its vulnerability once it is no longer protected from predators by a powerful parent group; yet the innate conflicts of interest when newspapers become in effect the puppets of conglomerates militates against the very editorial freedom that makes such diversity meaningful in more than mere statistical terms.

The shrinking Street

How the number of newspapers published in Fleet Street has declined since the 1920s

1928   Westminster Gazette absorbed by Daily News

1929   Daily News and Daily Chronicle merged as News Chronicle

1937   Morning Post absorbed by Daily Telegraph

1955   Sunday Chronicle closed

1959   Manchester Guardian became The Guardian

1960   News Chronicle and its sister evening paper, The Star, closed (absorbed by Daily Mail and Evening News)

   Sunday Graphic closed

   Empire News (Sunday) closed

1961   Sunday Dispatch closed

   Sunday Telegraph founded

1963   Sunday Pictorial renamed Sunday Mirror

1964   Daily Herald renamed The Sun (bought from IPC by Rupert Murdoch, 1969)

1966   Daily Worker became The Morning Star

1967   Sunday Citizen (formerly Reynolds News) closed

1971   Daily Sketch absorbed by Daily Mail

1978   Daily Star founded

1980   Evening News and Evening Standard merged as The New Standard (now The London Standard)

1982   The Mail on Sunday founded

Closed: 12   *Founded:* 3

Note: The Westminster Gazette, Daily News and Daily Chronicle supported the Liberal Party, the News Chronicle and The Star were Liberal, the Daily Herald and Sunday Citizen supported the Labour Party.

The Big Three

Total Sales, national dailies and Sundays   32,683,614*

	Sun 4,065,647	
	The Times........... .. 479.640	
	News of the World . 4,787,233	
	Sunday Times 1,257,709	
Murdoch	10,590,229	= 32.4%
	Mirror 3,271,861	
	Sunday Mirror 3,210,917	
	Sunday People 3,089,707	
Maxwell	9,572,485	= 29.3%
	Daily Express 1,875,291	
	Daily Star 1,434,562	
	Sunday Express 2,405,004	
Matthews	5,714,857	= 17.5%
	Total: 25,877,571	= 79.2%

* January-June 1985

Source: Audit Bureau of Circulations Ltd.

Chapter 3

Cheap papers cost dear

You left journalism a profession; we have made it a branch of commerce.
                    – Kennedy Jones, Northcliffe's right-hand man, to Viscount
                              Morley, statesman and former Liberal journalist

The national press, rightly, never misses a chance to expose, criticise or condemn the shortcomings of British industry – except, of course, those enterprises in which newspaper owners may have a stake – and to advise industrialists how to put their houses in order, step up productivity and discipline their workers, not least those of the nationalised sector. The tragi-comic irony of Fleet Street's exercise of this vital journalistic role is that however justified the target, however well aimed the editorial stones that rain down on inefficient companies and restrictive union practices, they are cast from the most fragile of glass houses, built on shifting sands.

What Kennedy Jones failed to say was that, thanks to Northcliffe, newspapers in future would operate on a commercial basis that applies to no other kind of business: newspapers sell at considerably less than they cost to produce and they have to sell simultaneously to two disparate sets of customers, the reader and the advertiser, in the right proportions, if they are at least to break even. In Britain we have the cheapest papers in the world, but at a cost that cannot be calculated in pence. Readers pay only a proportion of the cover price of their papers – the advertisers' 'subsidy' makes up the rest. Today a popular paper gets – or hopes to get – between 25 and 35 per cent of its income from advertising, while the qualities need a massive 70 per cent or more. And advertising is the most unstable source of revenue, the first overhead to be cut as trade goes into recession: when the economy sneezes Fleet Street catches a cold and the weaker papers tend to get pneumonia. Then only a rich conglomerate proprietor can save them – at a price.

When Alfred Harmsworth, a 31-year-old journalist and magazine proprietor, produced the first issue of his bright new ½d, half-price *Daily Mail* on 4 May 1896, using new cost-cutting machinery like the time-saving linotype, he changed not merely the face of British journalism but the economic structure of the newspaper industry. When that first copy of the *Mail* appeared there were already 16 dailies and 12 evenings printing in London alone, most of them, except for *The Times*, with circulations of only a few thousands, mainly in the metropolis, while another 150 throughout the country catered for regional readers. Most cost 1d (old money), although *The Times*, the Establishment's mouthpiece since the death of the great Delane, charged 3d. Until that time the daily paper was a minority habit – only about 16 per cent of the public, the middle and upper-middle classes, bought one – for they were mostly prolix and stuffy affairs and long, recondite leading articles that had little appeal or business reports, pages devoted to foreign, particularly Empire, affairs and long, recondite leading articles that had little appeal or meaning for working people. But Victorian technological genius and the growing need for a basically literate workforce to meet its increasingly more sophisticated demands provided all the elements for a revolution in Fleet Street: a new network of railways that reached into the most remote corners of the country, a telegraph system that linked almost every village with London, and millions of new 'graduates' of the 1870 Education Act, hungry for something to read but for whom the established dailies were too dull or esoteric to warrant the expenditure of a penny – that, after all, was the price of a pint of porter, the ordinary man's drink, and skilled craftsmen were striking for a wage of 9d (less than 4p) an hour.

That first issue of the *Mail* sold nearly 400,000 copies – almost as many as the combined sales of the other London papers. Harmsworth had hit on the formula that was to turn serious journalism into a minority taste: news in a palatable form for the emerging white-collar class, entertainment rather than indigestible Establishment information, women's interest features for that half of the population never before catered for by newspapers, and all at half-price. Harmsworth had plugged the cheaper-than-our-rivals theme in his widespread advance publicity campaign, but he diplomatically flattered his lower-middle-class readers' *amour propre* in the very first leader: 'The mere halfpenny saved each day is of no consequence to most of us. The economy of the reader's time is however of the first importance.' Not least he saw the reader as a customer for the new mass producers of processed foods and household goods, looking for the right advertising medium to expand their sales. The *Mail*, with its special page devoted to fashion, home hints, beauty preparations, diet, health and child care, was shrewdly tailored to their market needs. But in this perceptive exploitation of the reader as *consumer*, particularly the housewife, the biggest spender in the ordinary family, profitable though it was to prove for over half a century, lay the germ of Fleet Street's future sickness.

Four years after the *Mail's* launch he made his second break-through by starting to print it in Manchester; sales soared to just under a million, a fabulous figure in those days and still a large and profitable circulation in most countries outside Britain. The *Mail* was able to boast: 'This journal can be obtained each morning in towns as wide apart as Newcastle and Brighton ... *its advertising rates are higher than those of any daily journal in the English language and its readers the most numerous.*' The cheap *national* daily paper had arrived. Today Britain is still the only Western country of any size that has a wide selection of truly national papers, papers that are read the same morning from Penzance to Thurso. Harmsworth reversed the whole pattern of newspaper development as it existed in this country and as it still exists in other countries. Here the nine national dailies sell 15 million copies a day, more than seven times the provincial dailies' sales; in the rest of Europe the position is exactly the opposite and in the United States only three papers have a national circulation, calculated in thousands rather than in millions.

The immediate and highly profitable success of Harmsworth's innovations inevitably inspired imitators to scramble on to the ha'penny national bandwagon in a race for circulation that was to lead to cut-throat competition on a scale unknown in other countries: between the turn of the century and the present day some 22 national titles – including such old established and politically diverse papers as the Tory *Morning Post* the Labour *Daily Herald* and the liberal *News Chronicle* – have been killed off by the bizarre economics of the Northcliffe revolution. The battle for readers reached its pre-war nadir in the free gifts war of the 1930s when, in their desperation to win a lion's share of the market, the *Daily Express*, *Daily Herald* and *Daily Mail* offered everything from fountain pens, kitchenware and the collected works of Shakespeare, Shaw and Dickens to free life insurance to those who became 'registered readers' – i.e. contracted to place a regular order for the paper and thus boosted sales figures for the advertiser. Only the threat of approaching bankruptcy produced a truce in time for the press to cover a more serious war.

Peace in 1945 brought a decade of flamboyant prosperity that, among other things, launched the unions on a wages spree that has never ended, sending production costs rocketing, and, even more ominously, saw the introduction of two catalytic developments destined to erode the press's share of the national advertising budget, step up the struggle for that declining share, put more papers out of business and once again change the face of British journalism for the worse. The first, although its full impact was not felt for a few years, was the arrival from the United States of market research. Until then advertising had been largely a matter of personal salesmanship; obviously a mass circulation was ideal for washing powders, but much of the advertising was won either by high-powered space-sellers, a paper's reputation for 'pull' (Northcliffe's legacy to the *Mail*), or the advertising director's 'old-boy network' contacts. The *News Chronicle*, for example, lured its advertising chief from a rival paper in the Thirties and paid him a reputed £10,000 a year (say, £200,000 today) plus a Rolls-Royce and chauffeur, because of his undoubted influence with the agencies that place advertising. Market research, by analysing readerships and categorising them in terms of potential purchasing power – the A, B, C1, C2, D, E classes* – and measuring the paper's effectiveness in terms of cost per column inch (now column centimetre) shattered the old mysteries and started the polarisation of advertising between, say, the *Mirror* (then selling nearly 5 million papers a day) and the *Financial Times* (130,000 a day) at the other, specialist, end of the spectrum, leaving those in the middle like the *News Chronicle* – a widely respected liberal paper which boasted such famous by-lines as James Cameron, Vernon Bartlett and Ritchie Calder, but whose reputation as a good medium was revealed to be largely a myth – fighting desperately for what was left. This was bad enough but it coincided with the end of newsprint rationing. From the start of the war until 1957 the supply of newsprint had been pegged, and as this reduced papers to shadows of their previous selves millions of readers got into the habit of buying several dailies. Not only did this inflate circulations but advertisers had to queue up to get into any paper because of the limited page space. Inevitably, when in the mid-Fifties papers began to increase their paging again, duplicate readership began to decline and the gap between the successful and the weaker papers started to widen.

What the market researcher's detailed definition of a paper's readership profile did was not merely substitute his measurement of the readers' purchasing power and consumer habits for the cruder foot-in-the-door and lunch-at-the-Ritz sales techniques but, *pari passu*, without malice aforethought but nonetheless effectively, to undermine editorial authority even further. Editors had formerly

---

* A Upper middle-class (high-income professionals, executives, etc.)
  B Middle-class (middle-rank income groups embracing wide range, professional, managerial self-employed).
  C1 Lower middle-class (white-collar and other non-manual workers, owners of small businesses).
  C2 Skilled workers (tradesmen, foremen, etc.).
  D Semi-skilled, unskilled manual workers.
  E Pensioners and those dependent on social security.

shaped their papers' content and style on inspiration and flair, on their personal assessment of the areas of interest, tastes, educational intellectual and cultural standards of the public they sought to attract and influence; now the advertisers – or rather their middlemen the advertising agencies, studying the entrails of market research analyses – began to play a greater role in deciding, by their choice of the best medium for a given product, what papers would have to be like if they were to be economically viable. To oversimplify: if you sell frozen foods or consumer durables, from cameras to washing machines, you put your ads in the *Sun* and *Mirror* for blanket coverage of the household market, a total of some 50 per cent of the reading public; if you sell Rolls-Royces, capital goods like computer systems or share flotations you advertise in the *Financial Times* and the *Sunday Times*, which together cover only 10 per cent of the public but a concentration of the right kind of well-heeled, commercially important readers, attracted by their comprehensive and authoritative coverage of the business, financial and economic scene.

Advertising not only subsidises a paper's cover price but determines how many pages it will print on a given day: the size of the issue is not decided normally on the amount of news coming in but on the amount of advertising that has been booked. It is a vicious circle – with fewer ads, and therefore fewer pages, a paper appears to the reader to offer less value for money than fatter rivals; dissatisfied readers switch to other papers and the resulting fall in sales hastens the decline in advertising revenue. Yet the leftish *News Chronicle* and *Daily Herald* died 25 years ago not so much from lack of readers as lack of the right ads: both had circulations of over one million, a figure which in any other country, including the United States, would have put them at the top of the sales charts but in Britain's fiercely competitive national newspaper league is not enough to keep a popular paper alive at the going cover price. When the *News Chronicle* sought agreement with the other papers to a general cover price increase to offset the mounting costs of newsprint and, above all, production wages, that were hitting even the more prosperous titles, they refused. Within weeks of the *Chronicle's* death all the populars raised their prices: its demise suited them perfectly – it meant a bigger share of advertising for each of the survivors. Polarisation had claimed its first important victims. Some six million readers (on the calculation that on average three people see each copy bought) may have preferred their *Chronicle* or *Herald* to either the right-wing populars or the qualities, but the backroom boys of the advertising industry had served notice that it didn't need middle-range papers, however much their readers liked them, however desirable their continuance might be in the interests of diversity and political balance. In short, unrestrained 'free enterprise' market forces – overdependence on ads, costly overmanning – reduce the readers' democratic choice.

Almost simultaneously with the advent of readership research came another blow, the introduction of commercial television in 1955. Its impact on the newspaper-reading habit, further eroded from the late 1950s onwards by the quick growth of car ownership, is starkly obvious: over the last 20 years the total sales of the popular dailies have dropped by a million from 13.8 million to 12.4 million, with a drastic fall in the Sunday populars from 22 million to 15 million. In real terms the popular readership has declined even more sharply, for over the same period the population has grown by over three million. Even more telling, despite the steady increase in the national expenditure on advertising, is the degree to which ITV has siphoned off a growing proportion of it, sharpening the national press's struggle for its diminishing share. In 1956, when commercial television first got into its stride, the whole British press, national and regional, took 90 per cent of the news media's total £103m. By the mid-1960s, although advertising expenditure had trebled, the whole press's share had fallen to 65 per cent and television had overtaken the national newspapers, with 24 per cent of all advertising, compared with Fleet Street's 20 per cent. Today TV's share has increased to 30 per cent and the nationals' share is down to 16 per cent (1984 figures).

Fleet Street's share of the press's total is a relatively modest £677m, and a fifth of that is taken by the Sunday colour supplements (about which more later). A breakdown of the nationals' total gives a rough idea of their relative financial standing although there are glaring anomalies which shed an even more revealing light on their respective efficiency levels. Take the results of those two implacable rivals, the *Sun* and the *Daily Mirror* over a year. The *Sun*, with the biggest daily circulation, 4.1 million (which generates a huge income from sales alone), took £67.5m in advertising and made the biggest pre-tax profit of any national, estimated to be nearly £20m. The *Mirror*, second in the sales table with 3.3 million readers, won even more advertising, £71m, but ended up with a profit of £¼m.

A paper's managerial efficiency and productivity apart, circulation is no guide to profitability unless the readership profile fits the advertising agencies' specifications. Not only social grades but the sex and age of readers make up the profile. The *Sun* and the *Mirror*, with well over half their readerships under the age of 45 and by far the largest proportion of women readers – approximately 25 per cent each – dominate the nationals' advertising table;* for although only a quarter of their readers are in the top A, B, C1 bracket that proportion represents a combined total of some five million people who can be reached by the advertiser. At the upper end of the market the vital differences are greater and the position more complicated. Easily in the lead is the *Financial Times*, which took £55m in 1984 with a circulation of only 218,000, followed by the *Telegraph* at £52m, from sales of 1.2 million, more than five times greater. Well behind are *The Times* (£20m) and the *Guardian* (£17m), which both sell just under the half-million mark, with the *Guardian* marginally in the lead. Among the qualities the number of ABs, the two highest income groups, is important but even more important is the character of the paper. The *Telegraph* has five times more ABs than the *Financial Times* but it is in journalistic terms a quasi-quality, with a general readership, whereas the *Financial Times* has the status of a high-level specialist paper, aimed at the numerically small but financially influential sector, the male business world of the City and its equivalent abroad (only 0.9 of its readers are women).

Among the Sundays the two biggest sellers are Murdoch's *News of the World* (4.6 million) and Maxwell's *Sunday Mirror* (3.2 million) but Matthews's *Sunday Express*, with a steadily falling circulation – down from 4.5 million to 2.4 million in 25 years – still leads with the highest advertising income, £32m, some £10m more than either of the two leaders takes and a vital contribution towards its ailing sister papers the *Daily Express* and *Daily Star*. The *Sunday Express*'s 'pull' is enshrined in paradox: it is the last of the now unfashionable popular text papers, it has a much higher proportion of aging readers than its rivals, an editorial formula virtually unchanged since the 1950s and shoestring editorial costs but a higher volume of A, B, C1 readers than the *News of the World*. Second in ad revenue is Murdoch's *Sunday Times*, with £26m, exactly double the figure of its old rival the *Observer*. One indicator of a paper's pull is the price of a standard full-page advertisement, although competitive discounting often cuts official rates. Highest is the *Mirror's*, at £22,000, compared with the *Express* and *Mail*, at just under £15,000. In the quality field the *Telegraph's* £20,000 page is precisely double that of *The Times*. Well above all the other Sundays is the *Sunday Express*, which charges no less than £33,000, £7,000 more than the *Sunday Times* and four times more than its new rival, the *Mail on Sunday*.

If the competition for ordinary black and white advertising is fierce, the battle for colour bookings for the weekend supplements has become frenetic in the last five years as their numbers have doubled in the overcrowded Sunday market. Space salesmen now

---

* JICNARS National Readership Survey.

offer discounts of as much as 50 per cent to fill the colour magazines with the glossy consumer fodder that managements consider essential attractions in the battle for readers, even when their overheads – contracted-out colour printing is highly expensive – can neutralise their earnings. Once the *Sunday Times* – which pioneered the field under Roy Thomson in 1961 – the *Observer* and the *Telegraph* had what was then a very profitable corner to themselves. Today, despite or because of the fact that the editorial pages are often barely distinguishable from the ads, they are regarded as prime reader-bait in the 'something for nothing' approach to circulation building: no fewer than six now compete, with two of the later arrivals heading the revenue table: the *Sunday Express* with £36m and the *News of the World's* Sunday with £32m, followed by the *Sunday Times* with £31m, while the *Observer*, at £19m, and *Sunday Telegraph*, at £9m, trail at the bottom.

The relative success of the *Mail on Sunday's* relaunch after its disastrous debut in the summer of 1982 has been partly attributed to the giveaway appeal of its colour supplement *You* and companion comic. Yet although the magazine brings in almost double the ad revenue of the *Mail on Sunday* itself and the paper has reached a sales figure of 1½ million in only two and a half years – more than double those of either the *Observer* or the *Sunday Telegraph* – it is still losing millions of Associated Newspapers' money. The *Mail on Sunday* was designed, not so much to fill the crying need of *Daily Mail* readers clamouring for a full seven-day supply of their favourite editorial diet but to rationalise production costs by maximising the use of plant and manpower and at the same time weaken two of the *Mail's* daily rivals for the right-wing market. The strategy was clear: seduce *Mail* and like-minded readers away from the *Sunday Express*, the money-spinner which buttresses the struggling *Daily Express* and *Daily Star*, and also from the *Sunday Telegraph*, which is a financial millstone round the *Daily Telegraph's* neck. The plan to undermine them is working, although not as quickly as the Rothermere management had hoped. The *Sunday Express* had lost another 400,000 readers (13 per cent) by the end of 1984 and the *Sunday Telegraph* was down by the same percentage, 113,000 readers. But a circulation of 1½ million and a readership profile that includes many fewer A, B, C1s and women is still not a good enough combination to woo enough advertisers to put the paper on a sound financial basis: the *Mail on Sunday's* total ad revenue from paper and magazine was £41m compared with the *Sunday Express's* £69m. It will be a war of attrition in which Associated Newspapers' diversified interests, ranging from extensive and profitable North Sea oil interests and a provincial chain of 47 newspapers to furniture and transport firms, could in the end prove too strong financially for rivals which depend entirely on their own earnings. Whatever else, the competition for Sunday readers highlights a basic question of life in Fleet Street – can newspapers exist in their own right or only as branches of a conglomerate, with all that implies?

	Distribution of advertising revenue, 1964-84			
	National Newspapers £	*% of all advertising*	*Television £*	*% of all advertising*
1964	86m	20.8	102m	24.6
1969	111m	21.4	129m	24.9
1974	161m	17.8	203m	22.6
1979	347m	16.3	471m	22.1
1984	677m	16.7	1,245m	30.7

Source: Advertising Association

Chapter 4

The roots of junk journalism

I remember feeling sick when Neville Chamberlain over the radio described Czechoslovakia as a 'faraway country' and I remember expressing my revulsion to Lord Beaverbrook over the telephone. But when he said in a harsh voice 'Well, isn't Czechoslovakia a faraway country?' I agreed that it was and got on with my job of producing an exciting paper... That was the technique. Make the news exciting, even when it was dull. Make the news palatable by lavish presentation... the viewpoint that is optimistic.

       – Arthur Christiansen, editor *Daily Express*, 1933–1957

The metamorphosis of relatively healthy popular journalism into the junk food of the mass mind market has deep roots deriving as much from personal power complexes as from the fragile economics of the underpriced newspaper. The extravert *Mirror*, first under the earthy leadership of Harry Guy Bartholomew and then the equally robust but more perceptive and politically inspired direction of Hugh Cudlipp, blazed the trail that was to lead to a completely tabloid popular press, but it was Lord Beaverbrook's broadsheet *Daily Express* that in many ways pointed journalism towards the slippery slope which today ends too often in the gutter. If Bart's *Mirror* had the flavour of honest vulgarity, like the music hall, the Beaver's *Express* had a nasty, cynical streak. With its bold, brash make-up, huge headings and pictures, coy pin-ups, racy, sometimes raucous, editorial style and irreverent knockabout approach to the Establishment and all its works, the *Mirror* reached a circulation of five million by the 1960s and provided the basic blueprint of the literal shape of things to come. It was, however, the *Express*, with its ebullient, sophisticated and superbly presented journalism that made the deepest impression after the war on aspiring young recruits to national newspapers, fresh from sober, tradition-bound provincial sheets, and, notably, on the 21-year-old Rupert Murdoch when he arrived in Fleet Street from Oxford in 1952 to do an apprentice stint on the paper.

    Under the brilliant, idiosyncratic drive of Beaverbrook, né Max Aitken, the Canadian adventurer who had used his suspiciously quickly won millions to buy the paper and his way into British Conservative politics, the *Express* set the pace. Ironically, although he had acquired the paper as an instrument to further his ambitions as a Tory king-maker and to promote his bizarre and short-lived Empire Free Trade movement, it became, from the Thirties through to the Sixties, the brand leader of popular journalism, as seminal in its influence as Northcliffe's *Mail* had once been. The Beaver *was* the *Express*. Ruthless manipulator of men and news, he was a superb communicator who boasted to the Royal Commission on the Press that he ran his papers for propaganda not profit. Inevitably, they made handsome profits which he used not only to ensure that the *Express* had the biggest editorial staff in Fleet Street – more than 400 journalists – capable of swamping its rivals numerically on any story, but to bump up pay levels in the hope of pricing them into the red, whetting union appetites for bigger and better rises. Arthur Christiansen, an inspired editorial technician, was the nominal editor but Beaverbrook was the real editor, shaping the paper's every nuance by a daemonic barrage of orders, ideas, criticisms and, above all, prejudices that had no room for facts or fairness. His slick, synthetic product, almost entirely rewritten by sub-editors – the sub-editorial staff was by far the biggest of any popular – to a formula that adjusted the facts to Christiansen's dictum, provided its readers with an escapist view of the world through the vicarious delights of high life among the rich and glamorous and the constant assurance that 'you, too, can be a millionaire'. For Beaverbrook money was the root of all good copy. Yet sex was always treated with a curious primness: he affected a Presbyterian view of such matters while leading a private life of notable promiscuity.

As imitators had once rushed to follow Northcliffe's lead, so the rest of Fleet Street now tried to clamber on to Beaverbrook's spectacularly successful bandwagon and the cultural gap between the heavies and the pops widened even further. Northcliffe had brought the daily paper into ordinary homes by simplifying the traditional stodgy Establishment concept of news, widening the scope of coverage to include reports about everyday events and developments in the provinces as well as in the metropolis, entertaining as well as informing. He moved journalism down-market but in the best possible sense of broadening readership. When the then prime minister, Lord Salisbury, dismissed the new *Mail* as 'written by office boys for office boys' his aristocratic sneer was as ill-informed as it was snobbish. Northcliffe's staff included both graduates knowledgeable in serious affairs and recruits from his *Answers* magazine skilled in the sub-editor's technique of making the complex comprehensible and the esoteric readable. The *Mail* may have been the first pop daily but its parliamentary and foreign coverage would not be out of place in today's *Times, Guardian* or *Telegraph*.

Beaverbrook's *Express* was a very different cup of tea. Behind the black glass façade in Fleet Street the *Express* subs were not merely making the complex comprehensible but shifting the editorial balance from news gathering to news processing. Once a paper's reporting had created its character, now the reporters provided the raw material to be moulded to a prescribed formula by the very large team of top sub-editors: on the *Express* the ratio of subs (more highly paid) to reporters was considerably higher than that on other papers. The paper had some outstanding correspondents like Percy Hoskins on crime and Chapman Pincher on science and a handful of writers of the calibre of Cyril Aynsley, its chief reporter, but the by-line, which had virtually eliminated the anonymity of 'our own correspondent' in the interests of 'personalising' the paper, became an unreliable guide to authorship: when this writer offered his congratulations to a well-known *Express* specialist on his front-page 'beat' that day he replied wryly: 'The first I saw of it was when I opened my paper this morning.' The nameless sub had created 'his' splash story on the basis of a telephoned tip-off; it was a practice that was to become standard among the mass circulation papers.

The basic principle of Christiansen's formula journalism, shaping news and features to a predetermined 'exciting' image, prepared Fleet Street for the next generic change, the mass conversion to tabloid format. There is nothing inherently conducive to 'shock, horror, outrage' sensationalism in the physical proportions of the tabloid. The *Evening* (now *The London*) *Standard*, then a Beaverbrook paper and always tabloid in form, was edited with distinction for 17 years by Charles Wintour, who gave it an authority of style and a liberal-cultural reputation that belied its ownership and made it in many ways the equal of the qualities. But the runaway success of Rupert Murdoch's *Sun* equated success with size in managerial minds. It was obviously a more convenient size for commuters and, not least, it enabled a paper to charge more relatively for a full-page advert which was, in fact, only the equivalent of a half page of the old broadsheet. The truth was, of course, that the *Sun's* soft porn contents were even more important than the handy shape of the sheet in producing spectacular sales figures. No matter, within a dozen years all the popular national dailies and Sundays, with the single exception of the *Sunday Express*, had gone tabloid. Predictably, the switch to tabloid has failed to raise the sales of any convert to the smaller format except Murdoch's *News of the World*, which with even bolder projection of its sex and crime staple has climbed back to 4.7 million, the figure it last recorded in the 1970s on its way down from 8.2 million in 1952.

What the changeover did do was present impatient and worried proprietors and their hard-pressed editors with the ideal context for junk journalism. The traditional broadsheet popular, even when make-up became bolder, was essentially a text newspaper. Headings and pictures took up between 30 and 40 per cent of the average page, which contained some 4,000 words – enough to develop several detailed stories and in, say, average-size papers of 16 to 24 pages, offer the reader coverage of a wide selection of news and features to cater for varying tastes. In the down-market tabloid the packaging has become at least as important as the content: the massive monosyllabic headlines in WAR DECLARED! sanserif type and huge pictures can take up to two-thirds or more of a page, leaving space for barely 700-800 words. Front pages, in their desperation to grab the casual buyer by the eyeballs, frequently have room for only 200 words or less. It is a format which demands a degree of oversimplification perfectly suited to the dramatisation of the trivial and the sordid into the sensational. This visual con-trick has another dimension or, rather, a lack of it. The tabloid equivalent of the regular 16-24 page issues of the broadsheet would be papers of 32 to 48 pages: rarely in fact do the tabloids run to more than 32 pages. Today's tabloid reader is getting short weight in more senses than one. This physical transformation of the popular paper has not merely widened the visual difference between the tabloids and the qualities but their whole approach to journalism. The fundamental contrast between their respective newsgathering and editing techniques can be summed up in a phrase: the tabloid is a sub-editors' paper, the quality a reporters' paper.

Qualities not only seek to present the widest range of news and features, political, industrial, business, economic, social, home and foreign, sport and leisure, but to establish their characters and appeal through the individual style and authority of their writers, whether reporters, or foreign and other specialist correspondents or commentators. The sub-editor is an important back-stop who checks and, where necessary, modifies copy in the light of other relevant information, 'marries' different strands of the same story and cuts it into the space allotted in accord with its relative value on the night. Almost invariably, the editor of a quality is a former *writing* journalist, as distinct from rewriting sub-editor.

Popular papers concentrate more and more on specific news-gathering within their formula. At the lower end of the tabloid market the news editors and their regional correspondents and stringers – local journalists on retainer – look primarily for stories with a sensational theme, preferably involving sexual scandal or crime, popular 'celebrities' or public figures, either ready made from the courts or that can be 'developed' by interviews obtained if necessary by constant door-stepping, or otherwise dogging and harassing the quarry to check on his or her movements, and when the story is considered juicy enough, lavish chequebooking. Here the reporter's literary style is less important than his/her ability to dig out the dirt, in as much lurid detail as possible. On such a tabloid it is the subs, under the immediate direction of the 'back bench' an *Express* innovation, an all-powerful caucus of senior executives headed by the night editor, who rewrite, shape and beef up the copy in a highly-skilled process of synthesis that places great importance on bold, exaggerated layout. Straight news has to be a dramatic happening in the 'action' class – terrorist bombings, plane hijackings, hold-ups, train crashes – to oust a good scandal from the splash position. The tabloid editor has graduated from the subs' bench, skilled in the mechanics of presentation.

In effect it is the back bench that determines what goes into a popular paper on any given night, subject of course to overall policy. Notoriously, back benches, being by nature sedentary and limited by their working hours – from early afternoon to after midnight – to the company of their peers, in pubs and Press Club, and with little experience of the wider world outside newspapers, are conditioned to produce their papers with an eye to each other rather than for the readers under the knee-jerk reflex known as 'competition'. As the flow of news is highly variable, both in quality and quantity, and there might not be an obvious candidate for the lead story on the given night, when advertising bookings have decreed a big paper, the resulting issue of a tabloid can depend more on sub-editorial creativity than on the actual occurrence of any real events. On such a 'thin' night, the qualities will solve the problem by giving several reports more or less equal prominence across page one, with no one story dominating the page either in size of type or position. No such subterfuge is available to the tabloid: one story must be given the full treatment, fortissimo, all stops out, however slender its provenance. Under these circumstances and the pressures of edition deadlines, back benches have been known to change over to each other's lead stories after the rival first edition copies have been rushed across the street and conned nervously to see what the opposition have splashed. Another paper's story may be 'lifted', hastily rewritten to cover its origins, substantiated if possible by a quick telephone call and rushed into the next edition, whether or not, to save face and stave off criticism and loss of face, or worse, at the news conference post mortem the following day. The fact that a paper's readers would never miss what they did not know about does not figure in Fleet Street's warped concept of competition: the Pavlovian response to the threatening stimuli of the 'miss' is as deeply engrained as the touching belief that the word 'exclusive' is the sovereign remedy for all circulation ills.

It is sadly typical of the parochial approach to national newspaper journalism that such a neurotic and incestuous rivalry, like 'spoiling', another manifestation of the same anxiety, should take up editorial energies that in a more civilised press would be profitably engaged in establishing a paper's individualism. 'Spoiling' is the standard technique of rapidly cobbling up a carbon copy version, however faint, for simultaneous publication whenever a rival paper announces that it has secured an 'exclusive' series on, say, the love tangles of the stars of *Coronation Street* or *Dallas* or *Dynasty*, the 'secret life' of a gay rock millionaire or another of the thousand and one permutations of the sex-and-showbiz repertory that alternates with royal 'revelations' to fill the tabloid middle-spreads. This ingenuous manoeuvre to prevent the presumed desertion of readers to the rival sheet, inevitably heralded by hyperbolic publicity, including last-minute television commercials, plumbed the depths of banality earlier this year when Robert Maxwell, publisher of the *Mirror*, took the *Sun* to court over its attempt to 'spoil' the *Mirror's* exclusive serialisation of Peter Bogdanovich's book, *The Killing of the Unicorn*, based on the murder in 1980 of Dorothy Stratten, a *Playboy* magazine *'Playmate of the Year'*, who was killed by her estranged husband after her affair with Bogdanovich. Maxwell – who had declared portentously on taking over the *Mirror* that it would not compete in the soft porn market – first obtained an injunction prohibiting the *Sun* from using any extracts from the book following its announcement that it too would be telling the full story of 'the love feud of the century'. When the *Sun* published a 19-word extract from the book Maxwell accused it of contempt of court. The judge ruled, however, that the extract did not contravene the 1956 Copyright Act and ordered the *Mirror* to pay costs, estimated at £50,000. Kelvin MacKenzie, editor of the *Sun*, hailed the judge's decision as 'a great victory for the *Sun*, and warned that there would be no truce with the *Mirror*: 'Spoiling,' he declared triumphantly, 'is a legitimate part of tabloid journalism'. Legitimate perhaps, but a bastard deformation of genuine journalistic competition that has helped to turn the *Sun*, *Mirror* and *Daily Star* into clones of the same elementary cell.

No aspect in the change of the popular paper's character, accelerated by conversion to tabloid, has been more fundamental, or more regrettable, than the virtual disappearance of the staff foreign correspondents whose regular coverage of the international scene provided yesterday's readers with a wider perspective of the shrinking world. Extensive reporting of overseas news was not a monopoly of the qualities in the first 30 post-war years: it should be remembered that the late James Cameron, the outstanding journalist of that era, spent most of his distinguished career working for two popular papers – first for the *Daily Express* (from which he resigned because of Beaverbrook's increasingly malicious political line) and then for the *News Chronicle*. Significantly, Cameron then moved into television, which with radio now provides the mass audience with practically its only serious insight into the world abroad through its regular and excellent current affairs and documentary programmes. Today's tabloids devote little of their textual mini-space to any foreign news that is not either spicy or superficial: Jon Pilger's coverage of the Third World for the *Mirror* is a rare exception underlining the insularity of the general rule. The sub-editorial chauvinism of the *Sun's* 'Hop off, you Frogs!' campaign during the so-called lamb war with French farmers has replaced the wide-ranging, interpretative on-the-spot reporting of such popular paper by-liners as Cameron, his Washington colleague, the late Bruce Rothwell, and William Forrest, all of the *News Chronicle*, Donald Wise of the *Mirror*, René McColl and George Gale of the *Express*, and Christopher Dobson of the *Mail*.

The reason offered by managements is that the relative weakness of a fluctuating sterling and the high cost of communication make permanent bureaux abroad prohibitively expensive. It is true that the overheads of say, a full-time correspondent in Moscow, at least £50,000 a year excluding the journalist's salary (and just about the cost of a top linotype operator), take a large slice out of the editorial budgets of the *Guardian* and the *Daily Telegraph*, both of which stand or fall as individual newspapers, without the back-up resources of a supportive conglomerate. From the accountant's viewpoint, foreign coverage has always been costly, taking a proportionally large slice of the news-gathering budget; foreign editors, looking at it from the truer editorial perspective, have resented the fact that its scope has been limited by the much larger slice of overheads consumed by featherbedded unions. However, the real reason for the decline of the foreign correspondent lies less in Fleet Street's financial straits than in its personality change: foreign news that demands regular space to justify its cost does not fit into the mini-text formula of the tabloid with limited paging. If a major story breaks in Tokyo that cannot be ignored, the stringer's version may not be authoritative but it can be suitably stiffened with agency reports and dramatised by the imaginative skills of a top sub who may never have travelled further than Majorca, and who may be under the impression that the Japanese Diet has something to do with raw fish, but who is a wizard with raw copy.

On the home coverage side, too, a look at the number and type of specialists in the two branches of the national press reveals a quantitative difference that highlights the growing qualitative contrast between the serious papers and the tabloids. For one thing, the qualities employ many more specialists – more than double the populars' numbers in most cases. At least half of those writing for the tabloids concentrate on subjects that appeal to the advertiser no less than to the consumer (notably show business, in its many manifestations) while in the qualities – with the exception of the *Telegraph*, which in some senses is more of a quasi-quality – the great majority of specialists deal with news-related topics. To take one example: the *Sun* has some 15 special correspondents, several of whom double up in similar fields, mostly consumer oriented, while *The Times* and the *Guardian* both have over 50 each, three-quarters of them dealing with non-consumer matters. Consumer coverage, if handled with *Which?* magazine objectivity, can be an important service to the public, as television has shown in both BBC and ITV regular series; too often in newspapers, both quality and popular, it is the editorial back door through which the fast-growing public relations industry (see chapter seven) infiltrates its clients' puffs and plugs.

Circulation trends over the last 25 years

Popular dailies	1961	1985 (Jan-June)	
Mirror	4,561,876	 3,271,861	% Change
Daily Express	4,328,524	 1,875,291	
Daily Mail	2,610,487	 1,828,068	
Daily Herald	1,361,090	.... Sun 4,065,647	
Daily Sketch	981,698	... Daily Star 1,434,562	
	13,843,675	12,475,429	-10

Quality dailies			
Daily Telegraph	1,361,000	 1,221,092	
The Times	253,441	 479,640	
Guardian	245,056	 486,984	
Financial Times	132,928	 229,423	
	1,992,425	2,417,139	+21

Popular Sundays			
News of the World ..	6,643,287	 4,787,233	
Sunday People	5,450,727	 3,089,707	
Sunday Mirror	5,306,246	 3,210,917	
Sunday Express	4,457,528	 2,405,004	
Sunday Citizen	310,369	Mail on Sunday 1,605,228	
	22,168,157	15,098,089	-32

Quality Sundays			
Sunday Times	967,060	 1,257,709	
Observer	715,238	 745,692	
Sunday Telegraph	222,299	 689,556	
	1,904,597	2,692,957	+41

Source: Audit Bureau of Circulations Ltd.

Chapter 5

The Wolfe pack goes in for the kill

> *You cannot hope*
> *to bribe or twist,*
> *thank God! the*
> *British journalist.*
> *But, seeing what*
> *the man will do*
> *unbribed, there's*
> *no occasion to.*

– Humbert Wolfe

The most depressing aspect of Wolfe's witty, scathing stanza is that its eight-line indictment is even more justified today than when he wrote it more than half a century ago. Then journalistic excesses were largely confined to the political field and the greater diversity of national newspapers tended to balance the more biased views and angled coverage of the *Daily Express* and *Daily Mail*. Since the second world war there has been a demonstrable sharpening of pro-Conservative bias – a trend that will be examined later – but the heightening pressures of the struggle for circulation have generated a parallel decline in general journalistic ethics that is even more fundamentally serious in that the corruption of editorial standards inevitably contributes to a lowering of public tastes and attitudes, a blunting of sensibility and awareness of the real issues facing society, among millions of readers; in short, to debasement of the general culture.

From the turn of the 1960s the Press Council has sought, Canute-like, to stem successive waves of editorial anarchy and a new ruthlessness of method as the brasher populars fight – sometimes literally – for the kind of sensational and titillating 'exclusives' they believe will bolster sagging sales against the periodic advertising famine that reflects the wider national economic instability. The decline in news-gathering standards is wide-ranging and breaches both the Council's guidelines and the National Union of Journalists' code of conduct: from open chequebook journalism of the Christine Keeler and Great Train Robbery 'memoirs' type to 'body snatching' (when one paper physically prevents rival reporters from approaching someone whose story it has bought up); revealing against their wishes the identity of people involved in transplant, test-tube baby and similar medical cases; intrusion into private lives for the 'dirt' where there can be no mitigating plea that it is in the public interest; harassing bereaved and emotionally disturbed citizens in the search for quotes; 'adapting' interviews to make a headline or fit the paper's policy; even inventing news when the occasion demands.

The Radcliffe Tribunal, set up in 1963 to investigate press allegations about Admiralty and ministerial security after the Vassall spy trial, concluded that reports in several papers had been 'fabricated' and revealed that in some cases the journalist's only 'source' had been a report in another newspaper. Two journalists went to jail rather than reveal their sources to the tribunal. The most blatant case of fabrication brought to light since then was the *Sun's* notorious 'world exclusive' interview with Mrs Marica McKay, widow of a Falklands VC, which the Press Council denounced as a 'deplorable, insensitive deception on the public'. In a two-page feature the *Sun* reported: 'A VC's widow fought back her tears last night and said "I'm so proud of Ian. His name will remain a legend in the history books for ever".' A Press Council investigation revealed that in fact Mrs McKay had never spoken to the *Sun*, but only to the *Daily Mirror*, which had published an interview with her on the same day. In his evidence the managing editor of the *Sun* threw further light on the lengths tabloids will go to under the heading 'competition'. He claimed that the *Mirror* had had Mrs McKay 'under its protection' and refused to let other reporters talk to her. He denied that the quotes were fabricated; they came, he said, from stories in the *Mirror* and the *Express*, unscreened parts of an ITN film and an interview with the VC's mother.

The popular press's contemptuous disregard for the Press Council's moral, but unenforceable, authority became evident soon after it was set up in 1953, following the recommendations of the 1947 Royal Commission on the Press, which had been disturbed by the first signs that rogue papers were not prepared to play by the unwritten rules. The written ones didn't fare any better. In 1966 the Council issued its first Declaration of Principle after the press's callous exploitation of the horrific Moors Murders trial of Ian Brady and Myra Hindley, during which it was revealed that the chief witness for the prosecution had received weekly payments from a newspaper for information about the case. The Declaration warned that papers should not pay witnesses, actual or potential, and that 'no payment should be made for feature articles to persons engaged in crime or other notorious misbehaviour *where the public interest does not warrant it*' (author's italics). That last phrase provided an escape clause that editors have since been citing disingenuously every time their paper has been accused of chequebook methods. The appeal – for the Council cannot order – made little impact on Fleet Street's practice of buying its exclusives from any source, however tainted – a practice not entirely confined to the tabloids. In 1979 the Council severely censured the *Sunday Telegraph* for what the judge described as its 'deplorable double-your-money' contract to buy the so-called memoirs of Peter Bessell, a former Liberal MP, while he was one of the main prosecution witnessess in the trial of Jeremy Thorpe, the former Liberal leader, on charges of conspiracy to murder. The contract, under which Bessell was to be paid £50,000 should Thorpe be found guilty but only £25,000 if he were acquitted, was condemned by the Council as a 'grossly improper breach of the Declaration'.

If anything, the Council's 1976 Declaration of Principle on privacy has had even less effect. This stressed that 'the publication of information about the private lives of individuals without their consent is only acceptable if there is a legitimate public interest overriding the right of privacy, not merely a prurient or morbid curiosity', and this time it spelt out that ' "of interest to the public" is not synonymous with "in the public interest".'

But the uninhibited pursuit of sensational copy at any price, literal or figurative, reached an all-time low in the populars' frenzied competition for every gory, lubricious detail of the Yorkshire Ripper's trail of bloody sex murders which provoked the Press Council's denunciation of 'lynch mob journalism' in 1983. When Peter Sutcliffe, a 35-year-old lorry driver, was arrested near Sheffield's red-light district in January 1981, suspected of murdering at least 13 women, most of them prostitutes, what one might call the Wolfe pack descended on West Yorkshire and to new depths in their frantic efforts to get hold of exclusives, by hook or by crook. As the Attorney-General, Sir Michael Havers, commented later: 'The media, with honourable exceptions, lost their heads.' He might have added that they also lost their last shred of journalistic integrity and civilised decency. Only Sutcliffe's eventual plea of guilty and official embarrassment over the triumphant police press conference to announce his arrest, which appeared to confirm that there was no doubt he was the murderer, saved the press from charges of contempt of court for trial by headline before the actual hearings began. Sir Michael finally decided not to press the charges because, he explained, 'it was not in the public interest that a very large number of editors and others should be paraded in front of the Divisional Court'. It is difficult, in fact, to think of any action that would have been more in the public interest, a salutary lesson for all journalists and newspaper proprietors who turn freedom into licence, although admittedly it would hardly have helped the normally cosy relations between Downing Street and its tabloid friends.

The Press Council, in a searing, exhaustively documented 80,000-word special report, with a later addendum, condemned the collective behaviour of both newspapers and some of the broadcasting media that had put Sutcliffe's chances of a fair trial at risk and it heavily censured specific newspapers both for the relentless harassment of people involved, however peripherally, in the case and for flagrant violation of the Declaration on chequebook journalism. As a result of its inquiry the Council found it necessary to extend its proscription to include payment to anyone associated with criminals. The report described the 'ferocious and callous harassment' of relatives and friends of both Sutcliffe and his victims by reporters offering 'blood money' for any background revelations, and condemned the 'particularly unwarranted intrusion' to which they had subjected Sutcliffe's wife and Mrs Doreen Hill, mother of his last victim, Jacqueline Hill, a 20-year-old university student. The same journalists who can write critical accounts of soccer hooliganism and vandalism behaved little better in the pursuit of 'human' copy. In a personal comment, the then Chairman of the Press Council, Sir Patrick Neill, QC, described the scene:

> Following the arrest Mrs Szurma-Sutcliffe took refuge in the house of her parents. This was at once surrounded by reporters. Notes were thrown through the door and a sort of nightmare auction took place as journalist sought to outbid journalist and rival offers were shouted aloud. For days on end the house was beset and those inside lived behind closed curtains. The day before the trial was due to open at the Old Bailey the hordes were back at the house. At a late hour Mrs Szurma-Sutcliffe escaped with her mother by climbing out of a back window and creeping through the muddy, back-garden. Her account of how, in order to avoid the ever-watchful media, she took the night train to London and wandered dazed through the early morning streets, reads like a passage from Dickens. Every day as she left court her vehicle was pursued by cameramen on foot, on motorcycles or in cars.

The Council's adjudications gave a detailed insight into tabloid mores. The *Daily Mail* was found to be guilty of 'gross misconduct' and condemned on several counts. Its editor, the recently knighted Sir David English, who persistently refused to attend an oral inquiry, said the report, had for three months concealed from Sutcliffe's wife that he had no intention of paying her any money at all although sums of £90,000 had been hinted at in letters. The alleged offers were described as part of an elaborate 'charade' designed to obtain an interview without payment. The paper was also found to have made payments of £5,000 to Sutcliffe's father and it was further censured for 'deliberate suppression of the facts' concerning the accommodation of himself and his family when the *Mail* hived them off in hotels to keep rival reporters away from them. It was also condemned for trying to buy the story of the prostitute found in the car with Sutcliffe at his arrest.

The *Daily Express* was censured for offering Mrs Sutcliffe £80,000 although she was clearly a potential witness, and the Council deplored attempts by the then editor, Arthur Firth, to mislead it by hiding that fact. It refused to accept his 'astonishing' explanation that he had 'forgotten' the offers. The *Express's* sister paper, the *Daily Star*, was censured for paying £4,000 to the prostitute in the car and condemned after the trial for grossly misleading the Council by concealing important information. Its editor, Lloyd Turner, who had proposed in discussions with the Council that the chequebook Declaration should now include relatives of criminals, had done so without revealing that his paper had in fact paid Sutcliffe's two brothers £26,500 – the largest sum paid by any paper in the Ripper case and to 'precisely the type of recipient' Turner had recommended should be banned from payment.

The *Sun* was censured for paying a potential witness £700 for Sutcliffe's wedding photographs and the *Sunday People*, alone of the Sunday press, was condemned for paying an associate of the murderer who had accompanied him on his visits to red-light districts. Following the trial the *Mail on Sunday* was censured by the Council for its 'deplorable' deal with Ronald Gregory, Chief Constable of West Yorkshire, who had been in charge of the murder hunt, to publish his 'Ripper File' within weeks of his retirement. Both the *Daily Mirror* and *Sunday Mirror* and the *Observer* were absolved of criticism. None of the other nationals was the subject of any complaint. Indeed, some of the incidents which incurred the Council's censure were first exposed by the *Sunday Times*, the *Guardian* and *Private Eye*, on the press side, and by Granada TV's *What the Papers Say programme*.

Those papers which had been condemned were not slow to record their contempt for the Press Council – which has no power even to compel offending newspapers to publish its adjudications – and to head off any attempts to curb their excesses following the public and parliamentary outcry, stimulated largely by the quality papers and discussion of the problem on radio and television. Sir David English of the *Mail* commented: 'This is a most unfortunate decision by a body which should be devoting itself to protecting the freedom of the press. Newspapers, for all their faults, are the true guardians of the public interest.' The *Daily Star* declared that it 'was not prepared to accept any further restrictions on the freedom of the press'. Money that had been paid for information, it claimed, had 'helped to get at the truth'. The *Express* warned 'We should beware of attempts to manipulate the public's understandable concerns into a campaign for legislative restraints on the press.' They had little cause to worry: their collective counter-campaign and distorted accounts of a subsequent, unsuccessful, parliamentary move to establish a more effective statutory body, with the power of judicial sanction, effectively neutralised such 'threats to the freedom of the press'. As judge, jury and defence counsel in its own case, Fleet Street is in a unique and powerful position to secure its own acquittal in the dock of public opinion.

Chapter 6

Reds under the editor's chair

> ... *the evidence we have does not suggest that in either the national or the regional press at present the balance against Labour is a strong one.*
>   – Report of the Royal Commission on the Press, 1977

If the drift towards the gutter and the subordination of news content to sensation, scandal, jazzy packaging and million-pound bingo in the scramble for sales have provided the most dramatic evidence of the tabloid revolution's radical impact on popular journalism, the sharpening tone of explicit political bias has been no less serious in its effect on the quality of information essential to a healthy democracy: in the hands of the new press barons Fleet Street is markedly more unrepresentative of the electorate which buys its papers by the million than ever before. A newspaper without firmly held convictions would be as stimulating as a Prestel summary on the television screen. Partiality is a legitimate exercise of editorial choice, but over the last decade it has degenerated into naked prejudice without principle. The crude oversimplification of the tabloids' junk journalism, with its graffito-style headlines and minimal text, is complemented by the equally crude counterfeit of political views passed off as news. For millions of Left, Centre and agnostic Don't Know readers there is no longer any real choice of newspaper.

C P Scott and James Cameron spelt out the journalist's responsibility to the reader in their disparate ways. Scott, who turned the provincial *Manchester Guardian* into a powerful international voice during his 57 years as its editor, put it this way: 'The newspaper is of necessity something of a monopoly, and its first duty is to shun the temptations of monopoly ... Neither in what it gives, nor in what it does not give, nor in the mode of presentation, must the unclouded face of truth suffer wrong. Comment is free but facts are sacred.' Cameron's credo was less canonical, more personal, but no less to the point: 'It never occurred to me to be other than subjective, and as obviously so as I could manage to be ... I always tended to argue that objectivity was of less importance than the truth ... The journalist is obliged to present his attitude, to be examined and criticised in the light of every contrary argument, which he need not accept *but must reveal*. Surely the useful end is somehow to encourage an attitude of mind that will challenge and criticise automatically, thus to destroy or weaken the built-in advantages of all propaganda and special pleading – *even the journalist's own*' (this author's italics).

Both dicta beg the question of what are 'facts' and 'truth', but their central message has become even more pertinent in the degenerating climate of the 1980s: the fair presentation of both or various sides of a case is the essential prerequisite of a responsible newspaper's right to beat the drum of its own dogma. The misuse of proprietorial power to further personal advantage and prejudice is nothing new, but what was once limited to occasional outbreaks by a minority of Fleet Street owners has become the routine norm. When Humbert Wolfe, senior civil servant and minor poet, summed up the current state of the national press so succinctly, Stanley Baldwin, the Prime Minister, was publicly lashing the two leading press lords of the day, Beaverbrook and Rothermere – Northcliffe's brother and successor – for turning their papers, the *Express* and the *Mail*, into 'engines of propaganda for the constantly changing policies, desires, personal wishes, personal likes and dislikes of two men'. In a memorable phrase, minted for him by his cousin, Rudyard Kipling, Baldwin proclaimed: 'What the proprietorship of these papers is aiming at is power, and power without responsibility – the prerogative of the harlot throughout the ages.' Baldwin was hardly a disinterested critic, for both papers were campaigning for his removal from office, but he was right nevertheless. In the robust tradition of the 19th century, earlier newspapers had never minced their words, but Beaverbrook and Rothermere introduced a new, nasty and unscrupulous self-interested note to British journalism as their appetite for political power grew in ratio to the rising circulations of their newspapers. In 1924 Rothermere's *Mail* had published and exploited the forged Zinoviev Letter, purporting to be from the Communist International and linking Labour, by inference, to Moscow. Rothermere's obsessive fear and hatred of Communism bred a fervent admiration for Hitler and Naziism, as the bulwarks against Bolshevism, that permeated the columns of the *Mail*. And he was explicitly anti-Semitic: in a personal article in 1933 praising Hitler's 'new Germany' he attacked the 'Israelites of international attachments'. Only the withdrawal of advertising, by Jewish-owned firms in particular, muted this aspect of the *Mail's* editorial line, but not its advocacy of Naziism as a movement that would 'cleanse' a decadent Europe. The following year he greeted the formation of Sir Oswald Mosley's British Union of Fascists with another signed article headed 'Hurrah for the Blackshirts!'

Beaverbrook was no admirer of fascism but his political bias and personal malevolence towards political opponents and figures in public life tainted the paper's coverage. To keep business in buoyant mood and, therefore, continuing to advertise in the *Express*, he kept the slogan 'There will be no war this year' across the top of page one until within a few weeks of the outbreak of war in 1939. After the war the *Express* greeted Labour's election success in 1945 with an infamous front-page banner heading branding it as a 'national socialist' victory in a despicable attempt to smear the new Attlee government with Nazi connotations. It followed this attack up with a campaign that attempted to link John Strachey, a left-wing member of the government, by implication with the activities of Klaus Fuchs, a Communist atom spy. Nor was the *Mail* less virulent in its attempts to stigmatise the Labour Left as fellow-travellers and Reds, extremists who owed their loyalty to Moscow rather than Britain, with a diligence that would have commended itself to the first Viscount Rothermere, who had been succeeded by his son. The *Daily Mirror* responded in kind in the 1951 election with its 'Whose finger on the trigger?' attacks on Churchill, implying that he was a warmonger intent on a preventive assault on Russia. Churchill sued for libel and the *Mirror* settled out of court. The *Express* and *Mail* made much of this deplorable breach of journalistic ethics and resumed their campaign against the Left that has lasted for almost 40 years, intensified to near-hysteria during the 16 years of Labour's three terms in office but never yielding to any spirit of tolerance even during the long years of Tory rule. The *Mail*, in the tradition of its Zinoviev Letter ploy, has never failed to exploit any situation that might damage Labour's image, however insubstantial or even untrue the 'facts'. In 1977, when the Callaghan government was in office, it published a series of three articles accusing British Leyland, the nationalised car firm, of operating a 'slush' fund with the approval of Lord Ryder, then chairman of the National Enterprise Board. Ryder, said the *Mail*, had given his blessing to the bribing of agents, the breaking of tax and currency regulations throughout the world and deals involving illegal 'suitcase' money. When it was revealed that the whole series was based on a very clumsily forged letter allegedly written by Ryder, but which had never been checked with him, the editor, David English, apologised but denied that the articles deliberately set out to smear anyone. This was not the view of the Royal Commission on the Press, which – in contrast to the Panglossian conclusion of its main report – condemned the paper's 'serious misconduct' in a special addendum. The *Mail*, it said, had been 'a polemical and politically partisan newspaper for a long time ... what is novel is the extreme lengths to which the paper was prepared to go in an attack on the Government on inadequately checked information'.

By its nature routine political bias is less easily identifiable by the ordinary reader than the flagrant partiality evoked by elections, controversial legislation, strikes and intra-party rows of the Kinnock-Benn variety. The selection of certain facts, the omission of others that would modify them, the treatment of a story to impart an implicit rather than explicit emphasis, the prominence or otherwise of its position and presentation – all can contribute to produce an effect which the non-specialist reader is in no position to recognise let alone question. This built-in bias should, however, present no problems to expert observers, yet the last Royal Commission on the Press, which sat for three years, was able to produce the statement quoted above, with hardly the bat of an eyelid*. By definition the Royal Commission is an Establishment device designed not so much to provide radical critiques as to diffuse controversial situations by long-drawn-out deliberations that come to anodyne conclusions after the problem has subsided. This one was meant to be different, set up in 1974 by the then Labour prime minister, Harold Wilson, who was bitterly critical of Fleet Street's hostility and slanted reporting and anxious to find a way of balancing the bias of most of the press, possibly through some form of economic intervention that would encourage the founding of new papers. But in 1977 its report was in the classical tradition. It cleared the press of deliberate overall bias against the Left and the trade unions, although it conceded that coverage of the latter was 'a significant weakness' that should be tackled; rejected several proposed systems of subsidy and taxation to produce a more representative press; advocated steps to 'strengthen' the Press Council short of giving it any actual disciplinary powers; concentrated on six 'essential safeguards' to protect press freedom from the threat of the Wilson government's proposed closed shop legislation (which never materialised) and the journalistic monopoly this would give the National Union of Journalists; and concluded that on the whole the press meets the needs of the reader well, despite occasional falls from grace by individual journalists and newspapers.

Even the authors of the Royal Commission's bland report must have had second thoughts during the two general elections that

---

*Two members, David Basnett, then general secretary of the General and Municipal Workers' Union, and Geoffrey Goodman, industrial editor of the *Daily Mirror*, declined to sign the main conclusions and produced a minority report which said prophetically 'We do not believe it deals with sufficient strength and urgency with the dangers facing the British press. In terms both of the economic and democratic development of the press there are dangers that are apparent *now* but which in our view will become infinitely more so by the early 1980s.'

followed. At election time the partisanship of leader writers is a perfectly normal expression of the democratic process, but the cynical and explicit polemics that filled the 'news' pages of the popular papers – they were all tabloids by now – in 1979 and 1983 rubbed the Royal Commission's nose in its own report. To be sure, the one truth manifest in all party manifestos is that as prospectuses they would fall foul of the Companies Acts, but they serve as a basic litmus test of the press's general election coverage. Labour's mild 1979 manifesto, reflecting the cautious middle-of-the-roadism of the new premier, James Callaghan, was given the traditional Rothermere treatment by the *Daily Mail*. 'Jim's way: even more curbs' proclaimed the first of a series of banner heads that rose to crescendo as the paper warned about the 'wild men' who would take over if Labour were returned. The *Mail's* distortions stood out even in a field of such dedicated anti-socialist propagandists. Two examples give the flavour of the animus. Callaghan's remark, in answer to a question, that if necessary he would consider pacts with minority parties produced the huge streamer: 'I'll wheel and deal', with text to match. On the eve of polling day it devoted the whole of its front page to 'Twelve Labour Lies', lifted in its entirety from a Conservative Central Office handout, which denied among other things that a Tory government would double the VAT rate (almost immediately on taking office the Thatcher government raised VAT from 8 to 15 per cent). The *Express*, under its new owner, Victor Matthews, at least gave readers a well-displayed factual summary of the manifesto before reverting to Beaverbrookian attacks on the Bennite Left's sinister Orwellian plot that had 'laid down the foundations of 1984'. Its new sister paper the *Daily Star* – then in its larval 'independent' stage – filled page one with a factual objective account of the manifesto and kept up its fair treatment in its bid to woo much-needed Labour readers in the North and Midlands, then its circulation area. Alone of the nationals, the *Sun* did not consider the manifesto important enough news, good or bad, to displace its lead story, 'Sex prisoner locked in a packing case' – a headline that itself took up more than three times the space allotted on page two to the outgoing government's plans for Britain. In this one issue the *Sun* neatly illustrated the combination of sexual sensationalism, trivialisation of news values and political bias that adds up to junk journalism. Here it has to be recorded that, in sharp contrast, the qualities played it reasonably fair, keeping their views mainly to the leaders and political columns.

By the fourth year of her first term Mrs Thatcher's popularity had plummetted and her friends in Fleet Street were finding it difficult to disguise the message of the opinion polls when her rescuers appeared in the unlikely shape of Argentina's fascist junta. Historically, the right-wing popular press has always reflected and exploited the chauvinism bordering on xenophobia that was the British empire's principal legacy to working class culture, but not even the 19th century anti-Russian fever that gave us the word jingo or the white feather campaign of the first world war plumbed the depths reached by the tabloids in the few brief weeks of the South Atlantic action known since as the Falklands war. It takes real editorial courage to oppose the public mood, fed and whipped up by politicians and publicists of the Right, when 'national honour' is run up the Fleet Street flagpole, and those papers which took a stand against Eden's disastrous Suez invasion paid the price: the *Guardian, Observer, News Chronicle, Daily Herald* and *Daily Mirror* all suffered heavy circulation losses. Conversely, those which lauded Eden's ill-fated bid to teach the bloody Egyptians a lesson for daring to nationalise the Canal enjoyed a corresponding rise in sales for their patriotism.

It was no surprise, therefore, on 3 April 1982 that the four right-wing tabloids switched eagerly from bingo to jingo in a wave of the same brand of emotional nationalism that devoted as much space to the vilification of those who advocated the continuation of peace talks as it did to the real implications of a military 'solution'. 'Whose side are they on?' screamed the *Star*, which actually hired a lawyer to examine a Tony Benn speech to see if he could be charged with treason. The *Sun's* correspondent with the Task Force 'sponsored' a Harrier missile bearing the legend 'Up yours, Galtieri!' on behalf of his readers and the paper celebrated the sinking of the Belgrano, with heavy loss of life, with the notorious front-page 'Gotcha!' Infuriated by the efforts of General Haig, the American go-between, to secure a negotiated settlement, the *Mail* declared that Mrs Thatcher, until now its heroine, was behaving more like 'a tinsel butterfly' than the Iron Lady: 'Has she got the stomach for it?' it demanded angrily. The *Express* made no bones about Lord Matthews's war aims: ' ... nothing but a resounding victory is likely to restore the country's reputation and *preserve the Thatcher regime*' (my italics). Make the Falklands safe from Argentinian rule and Downing Street safe from Labour rule. Alone among the populars, the *Mirror* courageously repeated its Suez stand. 'Might isn't right,' it argued, warning against the dangers of the mounting war hysteria and the ultimate cost in British lives: 'The killing has got to stop ... if that means both Britain and Argentina need to compromise, then compromise they must.' It was the *Sun* that again touched the nadir with another attack on 'the traitors in our midst' – the 'pygmy *Guardian*' for one, but chiefly the 'timorous, whining *Mirror*'. Only at the end of its tirade did the *Sun's* commercial show through the simulated outrage of its hyperbole:

'We are truly sorry for the *Daily Mirror's* readers. They are buying a newspaper which has no faith in the country.' In short, be a real patriot and buy the *Sun*. It was a sordid postscript to an ignoble chapter in the not entirely noble history of British journalism, but the Tory tabloids' barefaced reinforcement of the old claim that the Union Jack is the exclusive property of the Conservative Party was an important ingredient in the creation of the Falklands Factor that sent the Prime Minister's rating in the opinion polls soaring again, ready for the real poll in 12 months' time.

The next election, in 1983, demonstrated even more forcibly that, whatever the betting odds at Ladbroke's, Labour faces the real odds of 14 to 3; of the 17 national papers, daily and Sunday, only the *Mirror* and its two sister Sundays actually backed Labour – but not its main policies, such as nuclear disarmament and withdrawal from Europe, as it stressed in the 340 words it devoted to the 20,000-word manifesto. The *Mail* gave it much more space, a two-page 'analysis' under a giant heading 'Britain in Bondage'. Condemning the 'most comprehensive assault on our liberties ever', a freelance contributor – who, piquantly, also acts as press critic for the Spectator – catalogued 80 supposed 'controls' on everything from the employment of baby-sitters to prices in an article of 1,700 words but not one about the main planks of Labour policy. So one-sided and unfair was the paper's coverage that *Mail* journalists held a protest meeting at which they voted to ask the editor, Sir David English, 'to give other parties a fair crack of the whip'. Deadpan, English retorted: 'It is unacceptable for anyone to try to influence the editor', which must have come as an unpleasant shock to his proprietor, the third Lord Rothermere. Never far behind in the auction for new readers among the hard-Right suburbanites who find the *Telegraph* too literate, the *Express*, with yet another new editor, Sir Larry Lamb, demanded 'Is Tebbitt too timid?' in a stirring call for an end to the trade unions' 'licence to misbehave' – a licence that is presumably the prerogative of tabloid editors. When Denis Healey took over as Labour front-of-camera man to compete with Mrs Thatcher's expertly contrived TV appearances, the *Sun* devoted a page of character assassination to 'The Beast of Pingle's Place' (Healey's country home) but gave a middle-page spread of pictures of male bottoms to maintain editorial balance and offset the charge of page three sexism. The *Daily Star*, now selling nearly 1½ million and reassured by the working class's desertion to the Tories in 1979, joined its *Express* stablemates in urging the return of Mrs Thatcher.

Although elections provide the most obvious evidence of the extreme lengths to which the Tory tabloids will go to defeat Labour by misrepresenting or playing down its policies, impugning its motives and its patriotism and smearing its candidates, their most rewarding source of sticks and stones is the industrial scene, where disputes and strikes can be used to brand socialism guilty by association. The exploitation of the so-called winter of discontent gave Fleet Street a ready-made opportunity to erode Labour support in the run-up to the 1983 election – with plenty of help from the more hara-kiri-minded unions themselves, it must be said. But the year-long miners' strike of 1984-85, with its long-running episodes of undeniable picket violence and massive, equally violent police response, and the abrasive personality of Arthur Scargill, relying on evasive rhetoric where frankness would have paid off, was a gift that the tabloids seized with glee in partisan coverage that fudged the real issues and provoked Fleet Street's print workers into controversial acts of censorship by industrial muscle. From the right-wing papers' viewpoint it was almost as 'good' a story as the Yorkshire Ripper and it ran much longer. This time the *Express* led the Wolfe pack. In a front page headed 'The truth that Scargill dare not tell' it printed a mock speech by the miners' leader which was in effect the *Express's* case against the strike. Bill Keys, general secretary of Sogat 82, the largest newspaper union, demanded that equal space be given to a reply by the NUM. Lamb, the editor, refused. Keys went over his head to Lord Matthews, who agreed to its publication. Lamb offered his resignation, which was not accepted. The NUJ chapel supported Scargill's right of reply but voted to black his copy unless Sogat withdrew its 'blackmail' threat to stop the paper unless it were published in full. Sogat downed tools and no London edition was published. The Press Council condemned the union for usurping the editor's freedom, but Sogat had made its point, however unconstitutionally: the NUM's reply was published.

Next to apply the smear technique was the *Sun*, which laid out its front page with a picture of Scargill, arm upraised in what the report described as a 'Hitler-style salute' under the heading 'Mine Fuehrer'. The print unions would not allow the page to be processed in that form and the paper appeared with a statement in bold type in its place: 'Members of all the *Sun's* production chapels refused to handle the Arthur Scargill picture and major headline on our lead story.' This was only the beginning. In one week in July 1984 the *Sun* failed to appear on three days, the *Mirror* and *Financial Times* on one day. The three papers were all stopped from publishing on the eve of the 'day of action' demonstration, organised by print workers in protest against Fleet Street's generally biased reporting of the strike, because they failed to print statements on the miners' case issued by the print unions. The other national papers which agreed to the unions' demand all appeared as usual. No journalist who cares about real editorial freedom can condone censorship by trade union walk-out: it is an unacceptable abuse of industrial power. But the deplorable disregard for basic journalistic ethics that has characterised the right-wing tabloid press over the last decade is itself an unacceptable abuse of editorial freedom. It is a problem that calls for more radical measures than the sincere but sanctionless censures of the Press Council.

At this point it must be said that the Labour Party and the trade union leadership must take a considerable share of the blame for gratuitously presenting a hostile press with so many sticks with which to beat them: the decline of the party's broad church tolerance, with all its faults and weaknesses, into fissiparous sectarianism more concerned with dogma than people; changes in the system for electing the leader which enlarged the power of the unions, whose card-vote clout and often dubious internal democratic processes leave them wide open to Tory legislators; the cynical packing of constituency committees, in the cause of reselection by union delegate-members whose own leaders often have life tenure; above all the use of strikes as a weapon of first resort, often with severe effects on the rest of the working class, and therefore on public opinion. The brutal truth is that any self-respecting independent national paper of the Left, if such existed, would have to investigate, report and comment on all these symptoms of the Labour malaise – without the distorting bias of the present press, to be sure, but also without any of the self-deluding whitewash that has no part in honest journalism or honest socialism.

It has long been conventional wisdom, enshrined in the pseudo-truism 'People never believe anything they read in the papers', that the popular press, because of its shallow, lightweight character, has no real effect on public opinion, least of all when it comes to politics. Even such a distinguished analyst and commentator on the press as the late (Lord) Francis Williams, himself a former editor of the *Daily Herald*, could say flatly that 'popular papers are without influence in political elections'. If they did have any real impact on the ordinary reader's political consciousness, runs the familiar argument, Britain would never have elected a Labour government. It is a simplistic argument based on the premise that election results are determined by the immediate campaign. Voting choices are obviously the product of a variety of influences, including the pendulum effect when governments run out of steam and into trouble, and, not least, the picture of society and the projection of selected sets of values presented day in, day out over the years to newspaper readers, many of whom have no yardstick other than the limited ones provided by radio and television by which to measure their favourite daily's continuous indoctrination. It could be counter-argued, therefore, that if the national press were more diverse, fairer, less fanatically pro-Tory in its treatment, not merely of overt politics and trade union affairs but of all important issues that are the stuff of implicit politics – education, housing, social services, conservation, health, etc., – Labour might have won power more often and by bigger majorities. It could be argued even further that, in an ideal world, in which a majority of newspapers were representative of the interests of the working class, the most numerous group in society, the Conservative Party might never have been returned to power again after the second world war.

Trade unions have frequently defended their resistance to postal ballot legislation on the grounds that their members, voting in the isolation of their homes, are more likely to be influenced by media distortion of the relevant issues than if they voted at meetings where their officials could present and clarify their union's case. On the face of it this might appear to be a sad commentary on the rank and file gullibility or, for proponents of the conspiracy theory, simply proof that voting by a show of hands among one's workmates, with all the group pressures to conform, enables the activist minority to manipulate the less committed majority. It is true that it is not easy to quantify the press's influence on voting behaviour, but a survey carried out by the London School of Economics election studies unit after the 1983 election offers scientific evidence of the part that newspapers play in forming political opinion. In an article in *New Socialist* based on its findings, Patrick Dunleavy, lecturer in politics at the LSE, concluded that there is a very marked correlation within social classes between the pattern of media influences to which people are exposed and how they vote. In the case of manual workers exposed to predominantly Tory papers, he pointed out, the margin of Tory voters over Labour was 17 per cent. Where manual workers were exposed solely to non-Tory media (eg the *Mirror*) the Labour margin over the Conservatives was 62 per cent. If one goes on to translate Dunleavy's figures in terms of newspaper readerships (estimated at roughly three times a paper's sales) this would mean that only about a third of the *Sun's* 12 million readers voted Labour although three-quarters of them are in the lower social grades. In the case of the *Express* and *Mail* only some 15 per cent of their combined readership, also totalling about 12 million, voted Labour, although just under half are in the lower social grades. Statistics, like news, can be interpreted to suit a predetermined verdict, but the LSE findings provide a clear indication that the monopolistic concentration of proprietorial power in Fleet Street is affecting the democratic process at its most vital point, the national ballot box.

Chapter 7

PR: The Fifth Estate makes news

A member shall not engage in any practice which tends to corrupt the media of communication.
    – The Institute of Public Relations code of professional conduct

PR is organised lying – Malcolm Muggeridge

While the most visible sign of the popular dailies' metamorphosis from broadsheet into tabloid has been the retreat from 'hard' news into magaziney pap (of both kinds), its strategic response to the challenge of the broadcasting media's non-stop flow of Newszak, the most insidious development has been the growing success of the public relations industry in insinuating its 'product' osmotically into almost every page of the paper. There are as many definitions of news as there are newspapers, from the Oxford English Dictionary's 'fresh events reported' to the 'man bites dog' apothegm, but fundamentally news is information you did not possess before. Whether you want to possess it is, of course, a highly subjective question: one reader's news may be another reader's yawn. Previously the populars solved this problem by offering readers a wide selection to suit varying tastes, ranging from the hard news of the day to the timeless 'human story' and pages of sport that carried all the results and racing form. Hard news is Fleet Street jargon for a happening that has occurred within a few hours of press time and it reflects British journalism's traditional preference for reporting 'action' stories, overt events, however fleeting their import, if any, as distinct from the much harder task of digging into the background of situations for their implications, investigating what may be carefully concealed or camouflaged developments and by revealing what is going on behind the scenes, who is doing what and why, make them real news – significant information. For the tabloids the trouble with so much of the so-called hard news is that television and radio can wrap up a story in a three-minute bulletin that gives as much detail – and probably later developments – as a page lead of 250 words that will be stale by the time it reaches the readers next morning, overtaken by a breakfast-time up-date. If indeed a late-breaking story ever reaches the readers in print – the prohibitive cost of replating a page, anything up to £20,000, means only the hardest of late news justifies a change.

As already pointed out, overt news, whether hard or 'human', is a fluctuating commodity, a fact of newspaper life that exacerbates the tabloid problems of early evening press-times and size predetermined by advertising, so the demand for ready-made early copy is strong. Enter PR: everyone, from the Prime Minister to the latest rock star, and not least big business, has something they want to sell, from ideas and personal images to consumer goods and services; it is an equation that the public relations industry has cashed in on at various levels. The unsuspecting reader is unlikely to have noticed it, but to the practised eye more and more of both news and feature pages bear the often well disguised print of the PR hand, from the 'Beauty Queen Drama' splash and picture filling page one to the middle-spread interview with Mrs Thatcher and the enthusiastic welcome in the City pages for the latest privatisation flotation. Fashion and show business may top the PR column inches count but no page is immune: every aspect of the consumer scene, household goods, food, health, baby care, motoring, gardening, travel, wine, electronics, and of course politics in all its guises – all are grist to the busy and profitable mill of what one might call the Fifth Estate, the creators of copy that is in effect subsidised, usually with a commercial profit in view, and, at its most sophisticated level, the practitioners of news management.

The Sage of Robertsbridge was perhaps pitching it rather strong when he damned PR as planned prevarication, but there is more than a scintilla of truth in his charge. The very phrase 'public relations' is itself a euphemism disguising the object of the exercise – publicity, *good* publicity, although the vulgar word is eschewed by the smoother practitioners. Basically, the aim of PR is to tell you what it wants you to know and to keep you from finding out what it doesn't want you to know. That is not by any means to suggest that all public relations people are liars; but the very nature of their function militates against the chances that they will often freely be volunteering the whole truth and nothing but the truth. That should be the journalists' job – revealing the truth as they see it and as far as they can unearth it. It is hardly coincidence that the decline of the old-fashioned virtue of digging for the facts instead of having them delivered on a plate has been in inverse ratio to the rise of public relations, one of Britain's few fast-growing industries.

When the second world war ended there was only a handful of public relations specialists, mostly former official information officers who had learnt their craft 'managing' the news – largely bad news for three years – for the government propaganda machine controlled by the Ministry of Information. Today there are estimated to be 10,000, almost one to every three journalists – a formidable ratio by any reckoning – and their numbers are increasing by as much as 30 per cent a year, according to the trade press. They come in all shapes and sizes: the single freelance doing one-off press releases for local firms; the in-house teams of major manufacturing companies with both product and industrial relations axes to grind; the large international groups which handle everything from the client's brochures and the chairman's speeches to press conferences, media campaigns and 'freebies' – free trips with lavish entertainment designed to put moral pressure on the recipient to write a friendly piece about the client's activities; and by no means least Whitehall's 1,000-strong phalanx putting out the government's version of the state of the nation, from the official gloss on the latest economic or unemployment figures and the Defence Minister's predilection for combat jackets to the Prime Minister's views on anything that might inspire a favourable headline.

It is big business: the 110 member firms of the Public Relations Consultants' Association, the body representing the more important independent groups, have a total fee income of £25m a year, with a total expenditure of some £500m that indicates the ramifications of the all-pervasive PR network. Thirteen consultant firms take more than £1m each in fees. These are the top specialists with plush London offices and international connections, offering what the PRCA's yearbook defines blandly as 'the effective transmission of messages from the company to the various audiences through a series of techniques that are varied, often subtle and rarely easy'. The consultants' 2,500 clients range from Annabel's, the West End nightclub, to the Oman Ministry of Defence, with every imaginable product and service in between, including Fleet Street newspapers and the Newspaper Publishers' Association. Several of the big 13 specialise in the political field and retain MPs and other public figures who both broadcast and write newspaper articles in their capacity as experts. Good Relations, numerically the biggest of them all, with 130 PRs on its staff, boasts no fewer than three Conservative MP-advisers, Sir Anthony Grant, Michael Mates and Peter Archer. Shandwick Consultants, whose services include parliamentary affairs, takeover bids and corporate crises, is headed by the well-connected Peter Selwyn Gummer. One of his directors is Lord Chalfont, one-time regular army officer and defence correspondent of *The Times*, Minister of State at the Foreign Office in the Wilson government, company director and frequent writer and broadcaster on foreign and defence affairs. Among Shandwick's many clients is International Military Services. David Wedgwood Ltd, which 'specialises exclusively in parliamentary and EEC affairs ... activities of government at local and national level . . . civil service and pressure groups', has one Conservative MP consultant, David Crouch, and an MEP, William Dunn. Another firm with political expertise is Identity Campaigns (UK), which cites 'privatisation programmes' among its activities. Not all consultants are as explicit as Neil Jamieson Associates, which 'publicises clients worldwide through the editorial columns . . . writing and placing specialised features', but that is what much of high-level PR is about. PR's links with Parliament were recently highlighted by the Select Committee on MP's Interests, which shifted its attention from the outside connections of Members themselves to the activities of some parliamentary 'journalists' who have access to the House's information sources and are suspected of being not reporters but employees of public relations firms who have acquired accreditation for their own purposes.

Today the head of a powerful conglomerate's in-house PR section or consultancy policy is an important member of the board, boasting a sonorous-sounding title such as Director of External Affairs, or Corporate Relations. A measure of the value that companies attach to such experts is that, as the PRAC reports, headhunters are now finding it difficult to meet the increasing demand from clients like banks and oil firms although the going salary rate is in the £40,000-£50,000-a-year bracket – the price of a Fleet Street editor. Most PRs operate at a much less grand level, but they have moved up from the gin and tonic approach, according to the Institute of Public Relations, the professional body representing individual PRs, which administers the 16-clause Code of Professional Conduct. This is an impressive-looking document, which among other things sternly forbids 'any attempted influence on the decision-making processes of the press' and specifically prohibits even such modest routine bribery as 'a case of whisky for an editor before – or after – he has published a story'. It says nothing, however, about providing him or one of his staff with all the drink he or she can consume on a sponsored free trip to some sunny fun resort or goodwill tour of a foreign regime in need of Western friends, or funds, which can produce the right kind of write-up in the Daily Puff. The scope of the freebie is wide-ranging. British Airways, which retains no fewer than three PR consultancies in addition to its own press section, recently flew a planeload of journalists to the South of France for the 'preview' of its new staff uniforms, with lots of coverage of this important development in aviation to show for it. At a less frivolous level, this writer once flew back from what was then Rhodesia in a plane that by chance was carrying a PR-sponsored party of MPs and other opinion-formers, whose chaperoned experience of the benefits of white rule in that country differed sharply from the realities of life for the Africans encountered by an unescorted reporter.

Many of the earlier PRs were hard-bitten ex-newspapermen, gamekeepers turned poacher and relying on their inside contacts, and many of the rank and file still are members of the National Union of Journalists. But the industry's growing affluence has encouraged its pretensions to professional status and today's recruits are often graduates – Cambridge leads among the top consultancies – and an increasing number of women are joining: 40 per cent of all PRs and 20 per cent of consultancy directors are female. With business booming the Institute has embarked on a 'much wider role' that includes the coaching of company executives in the art of dealing with the press and it looks forward to even greater expansion now that lawyers and accountants are being allowed to publicise their services. One of the Institute's claims is that clients of all kinds are beginning to realise that 'they get more for their money from a PR campaign than from traditional advertising'. What the client hopes to get, of course, is his advertising message put across in the guise of journalism. It is ironical, however, that no matter how effective it may be at creating and projecting attractive images, corporate or personal, for the client, PR has not been entirely successful in sloughing off its own reputation as a slightly spivvy, parasitic go-between occupation. Undeterred, the Institute is increasing its efforts to move its image up market. It has raised £105,000 to endow a chair of public relations at Cranfield College: next year will see the graduation of the first practitioners entitled to add MBA(PR) to their letterheads.

Much of PR is no more sinister in its effects than in the sense that it influences readers' choice by plugging, often under a staff specialist's by-line, the advantages of one type of product – say, the rotary as distinct from the traditional mower – that attracts more advertising than another. The specialist doesn't need to mention the product by name – the huge ad next to the article does that. What is serious, however, is the PR aimed at readers' minds rather than at their pockets, and it is at this level of propaganda that uncritical and sloppy journalistic practice compounds endemic bias and institutionalised unfairness. It may seem perverse to call the pot as a prosecution witness against the kettle, but Bernard Ingham, the Prime Minister's controversial press officer, regarded by some Lobby correspondents as more Thatcherite than his boss, was voicing a view held by some serious journalists as well as disinterested observers when he denounced the press for its 'laziness, laxness or arrogance – or a combination of all three' and its failure to search rigorously for the truth. 'I do not now find an unremitting drive to check', he told the International Press Institute last March, 'rather do I find an unrelenting drive to put two and two together and make 22 ... Facts, so it seems, are less than ever to be allowed to get in the way of a good story.' Naturally, the bitterness of Ingham's attack owed more than a little to sour grapes – the eagerness of even the government's most rabid supporters to exploit its second-term predisposition to banana skin gaffes and wet-dry splits must have come as an unpleasant shock after No 10's long honeymoon with Fleet Street, although as his predecessor there during the Macmillan years, Sir Harold Evans, pointed out in his memoirs, 'Lobby journalists can be very rough indeed, not least with prime ministers of whom they have become tired.' He might have added that it is a temporary phenomenon: the bored or disaffected political correspondents of Tory papers quickly rally to the colours at election time.

The piquant truth underlying Bernard Ingham's blunt Yorkshire outburst is that the laziness and laxness he so rightly castigates are engendered and encouraged by the selective spoon feeding he and his fellow PRs have brought to a sophisticated art form. The marketing of Margaret Thatcher on American presidential lines through the expensive skills of Gordon Reece, former journalist, TV producer and marketing director of EMI, nursery of pop stars, and Saatchi & Saatchi, the whiz kids of advertising, backed up on the day-to-day routine by Ingham, is a classic example of high-powered public relations manipulation of a complaisant press and television networks for whom pictures are a synonym for news. It was Reece who masterminded the Prime Minister's public, as distinct from parliamentary, personality change that transmogrified the shrill headmistress prone to bitchiness into the 'caring', smoothly styled mezzo-soprano of the television studio and substituted a programme of precisely structured media 'events' for the hurly-burly of the hustings, with its small audiences and the constant danger of heckling-induced gaffes. In both the 1979 and 1983 elections PR played a major role in selling her personal image rather than the nitty-gritty of Tory policies, in a series of slickly stage-managed tours of factories, farms and old folks' homes to press the flesh, pet cuddly calves and exchange housewifely banalities with shoppers on walkabouts, tactically timed for television news and tabloid first editions – all swallowed whole by the mass media. It was, in short, a cynically conceived exercise in projection before politics, the media appearance as the message – a masterly propaganda coup reported as news by an uncritical Fleet Street, with only the *Observer* revealing what was going on behind the Barnum façade of the triumphant Tory circus.

PR takes as many shapes as Proteus in its efforts to win friends and influence media people, from the tons of press releases and brochures it churns out weekly to Claridges receptions and patronage of all kinds, sporting, artistic, political. Prime ministers have been dishing out honours in return for favours, past or future – or, in Lloyd George's case, for straight cash – since the First Lord of the Treasury took over from the Monarch as the real power in the land. None, however, not even Harold Wilson, has ever bestowed them on Fleet Street with such blatant self-interest as Mrs Thatcher. No sooner had she won the 1979 election than she handed out titles to three unlikely recipients whose main qualification appeared to be the notable part their papers had played in knocking Labour – and the SDP Alliance, as secondary target – and getting the Conservatives in with a thumping majority: Victor Matthews, new boss of the *Express* group, Larry Lamb, then editorial overlord of Murdoch's *Sun* and *News of the World*, and John Junor, editor of the *Sunday Express* – all 'ennobled' in 1980. Matthews, unknown outside the Trafalgar House company before it bought *Express* Newspapers only three years earlier, was given a peerage and Lamb and Junor knighted. David English, editor of the *Daily Mail* and Mrs Thatcher's most fervent supporter, who had been expected to receive his reward too at the same time, had to wait until 1982 for his knighthood because of the political stink left by his paper's forged 'exposé' of the alleged British Leyland slush scandal in 1977 and the Royal Commission's indictment of its 'serious misconduct' in the affair. However, a week is a long time in politics and five years is enough to deodorise any smell among friends in the Third and Fourth Estates.

Yet what struck even Fleet Street cynics was the Prime Minister's cavalier disregard for the traditional proprieties in her haste to show her gratitude. Normally, peerages have gone to proprietors only after they have been on the newspaper scene for a considerable time, while editors and leading journalists have received their honours, if any, towards the end of their active careers, or later. Lord Astor of Hever was owner of *The Times* for 34 years before he got his title and Roy Thomson had to wait 14 years for his peerage. Hugh Cudlipp was knighted the year he retired after a lifetime with the *Mirror* group and made a peer the following year. William Rees-Mogg, editor of *The Times* for 14 years, got his knighthood on leaving journalism, Gordon Newton received his after editing the *Financial Times* for 16 years. Three editors who got nothing are Alistair Hetherington, who occupied the *Guardian* chair for 19 years, Maurice Green, editor of the *Daily Telegraph* for 10, and Fredy Fisher, who edited the *Financial Times* for seven. Even Harold Wilson, whose embarrassing choices for his Dissolution Honours list further tarnished what was left of his reputation, elevated John Beavan (Lord Ardwick) and Sydney Jacobson, both of the *Mirror*, only after both had retired from editorship, towards the end of long careers in journalism.

One of the most important subjects handled by in-house public relations sections employed, or independent consultants retained, by large manufacturing companies is industrial relations – regularly putting over the company line to the workers and, when disputes break out, to the news media. To underline the vital nature of this function, the Public Relations Consultants' Association has produced a very fair, informative guidance paper, *Understanding the Unions*. The trade unions themselves would benefit from an equally intelligent guidance paper on Understanding Public Relations. Obviously, most trade unions would be unable to afford the large and costly teams that multinational groups and nationalised industries regard as essential to ensure a good press for every aspect of their operations, from marketing a product to selling their side of the case when a strike hits the headlines. But on the analogy of the Salvationist philosophy that the devil should not be allowed a monopoly of all the good tunes, the unions, like the Labour Party, will have to stop bemoaning Fleet Street's built-in bias and relying on counter-productive censorship-by-stoppage by print workers and grasp the fact that PR is not the prerogative of employers and the Conservative Party if they mean to get themselves a better, if not a good, press.

As Patrick Wintour has pointed out in the *Guardian* – which itself has a reputation for balanced industrial reporting – the unions have been completely outmanoeuvred in recent strikes, notably the miners' year-long stoppage. The Coal Board, with over 40 press officers on its staff, set the agenda for reporters each day by producing its return-to-work figures by 9 am and followed up by issuing its own detailed accounts of picket-line violence, compiled with the help of police press teams. By mid-morning, he reported, these stories were on the news desks of both press and broadcasting media. The National Union of Mineworkers had one press officer to deal with the 100 journalists who crowded into its HQ for press conferences. And, as Wintour commented, Arthur Scargill, the mineworkers' president, merely parried questions, declared 'The strike is still on!' and failed signally to exploit the opportunities afforded him to explain the union's case and counter NCB allegations. 'The NUM leadership,' Wintour concluded, 'did not seem to come to the press conferences with any sense of what the union could gain from them.'

The miners' failure to put over their case from the beginning encapsulates the Left's inability to comprehend the nature of the age of instant communication and to realise that, given the hostility of most of the press and the inherently Establishment approach of television – Channel 4 and Granada excepted – public opinion can still be influenced by the intelligent and well-organised projection of reasoned argument, backed up by diligent research. One outstanding exception to the Labour-union norm is Ken Livingstone, whose masterly campaign to save the GLC produced a strong swing in his favour that exposed the ideological dogmatism of the government's plan. The hard fact to be faced is that Arthur Scargill's tactics were a gift to the news media in general and the right-wing tabloids in particular, eroding early public sympathy, as reflected in the opinion polls, as he harangued reporters and cameras demagogically where he should have been reasoning persuasively, always dodging the central question: 'Why don't you have a national ballot, according to your union's rules?' If a tithe of the millions of pounds lost over the 12 months by the NUM had been spent earlier on a well thought out and expertly researched media campaign, challenging the Coal Board's criteria on the fundamental question of 'uneconomic' pits and the government's failure to produce an overall energy plan, the mining community might have been spared the misery of its disastrous defeat.

It must also be said that although Arthur Scargill and his executive are outstanding examples of how not to cope with media bias, too many other unions and their leaders suffer from the same fatal blend of cliché-ridden rhetoric and defensive aggressiveness which plays into the hands of unsympathetic reporters and interviewers and provokes those prepared to be neutral if not helpful. One does not have to agree with Ken Livingstone's more idiosyncratic views and trickier political ploys to hold him up as a model communicator from whom both Labour and union leaders could take some vital lessons if the justifiably aggrieved Left is to make any dent in press prejudice before the great millennial democratisation of the media turns C P Scott's precept into practice. Livingstone exploited every aspect of PR projection, from TV, radio and newspaper interviews, media-covered speeches in every borough and cogent well-researched articles in any paper that would take them – all followed up with specially commissioned opinion polls demonstrating that three-quarters of all Londoners now supported retention of the GLC. His own television appearances squashed the tabloid-inspired image of the extremist Red Ken: disarmingly moderate and persuasive in tone, witty and invariably good humoured, confidently needle-proof, politely firm in making his points, better briefed than his interlocutors. What his opinion polls showed was that the majority of London ratepayers, including hundreds of thousands of Conservative voters and many of their councillors, could get the message if it were put across to them the right way.

The moral is plain: two sides can play the PR game. The Left may not win the immediate confrontation – as with the GLC – but it could effectively counter Fleet Street misinformation if it set out collectively to challenge the Right's virtual monopoly of public relations techniques with a continuing, concerted, positive and properly funded communications strategy in place of short-term tactics – acting instead of reacting. The Fifth Estate is a fact of media life that is here to stay. After all, the post-war Labour government recognised the challenge in 1945 when Clement Attlee appointed the first full-time Downing Street press secretary. It is time the Left got the message.

Chapter 8

Chapel power rules, OK?

If the 300 men on the strength of the machine room all turned up
for their shift there wouldn't be room to move, so we run the half-
night system, with half of the men working at any one time
– Manager, national daily paper

In Fleet Street the corrupting cynicism that can come with unfettered power is not the monopoly of the press barons: the erosion of journalistic standards and ethics by self-interested proprietors and their house-trained and easily replaced editors to meet the pressures of the circulation/advertising rat-race has been paralleled down the years by an equally self-interested distortion of the economics of production by a workforce that has played its part in creating the conditions for that decline. The national newspaper scene is a microcosm of the problems which the second industrial revolution poses for Britain, only more so. Its very structure, mores, history and the perishable nature of the product are a recipe for continuous confrontation between management and unions in a long-running conflict that is now approaching a climax over what, after nearly two decades of neo-Luddite resistance to its introduction, is still solemnly called the 'new' technology. On one side of the negotiating table sit the front men of the buccaneering egotists whose success in the cut-throat world of the takeover coup militates against both co-operation with their peers and the collective ethos of a socially responsible press; on the other side, the tough, tightly organised chapels whose internal solidarity, backed by a ruthlessness equal to that of any Murdoch or Maxwell, has yielded them such Croesian rewards for routine skills and semi-skills for so long that they find it impossible to adjust to the traumatic certainty that the goose which laid an endless supply of ever-larger golden eggs is programmed to join the dodo, killed off by the ubiquitous computer. The multi-million pound question now is not 'if' but when – and on what terms.

So far the employers have established four bridgeheads in the campaign to convert the national newspapers from the costly, outmoded hot metal process of printing to 'cold' setting: the *Mirror* Group, which began the switch to computerised photo-composition as early as 1976, when it 'bought the rule book' to secure union agreement; *Times* Newspapers, which completed the changeover in 1982, but only after the year-long lockout which led to their sale to Rupert Murdoch; the *Observer*; and the *Mail on Sunday*, cold set from its launch in 1982. It has been a slow, limited advance that leaves another 10 titles to go before Fleet Street can be said to have moved into the second half of the twentieth century. And even when all 17 national papers are setting their type electronically – and that could be several years off – that will be only half the battle to rationalise the top-heavy production system. For the brutal logic of photo-composition and its allied techniques is not merely that the cumbersome 19th century linotype and the thousands of individual metal 'slugs' it casts to fill a paper should make way for the sophisticated electronic keyboard of the VDU (visual display unit) but that the incredibly highly paid operators who tap out the slugs and their colleagues who assemble them manually in page form should also disappear with their machines into the history books and industrial museums like the cottage weavers, wheelwrights, sailing ship masters, car factory spot welders and other specialists overtaken by human inventiveness. The once vital skill of the typesetter – much overrated in its newspaper context as distinct from other branches of the printing trade – has been rendered literally redundant by the skills of the new breed of craftsmen, the computer designers, engineers and programmers whose ingenuity has provided a flexible electronic system that enables journalists and advertising staff to type their copy straight into the master computer – 'direct input' – ready for printing, type faces and sizes selected by the pressing of a key, thus eliminating the time-consuming and financially wasteful 'double keyboarding' in which editorial typescript is retyped, not always accurately, by NGA operators.

All five unions are affected in varying degrees by the implications of the new technology: the NGA (National Graphical Association), which organises the craft workers like typesetters, stereotypers, engravers telegraphists and the machine minders in the pressroom; Sogat '82 (Society of Graphical and Allied Trades), representing the semi-skilled in pressroom and warehouse, where the papers are prepared for distribution, and clerical staff; the engineers and electricians, who belong to their national unions and service the plant; and the NUJ (National Union of Journalists), whose members staff the editorial departments and create the newspaper. But it is the typesetters, the central core of the NGA, who stand to lose most, not only materially because they have always had bigger golden eggs than their fellow newspapermen, including the journalists, but psycho-logically through the erosion of their cherished role as the aristocrats of the production workforce. There is no love lost between the craft-conscious NGA and Sogat, whose members it tends to patronise collectively as a lower order of industrial society, although not often as bluntly as the father of a composing room chapel who habitually referred to them as 'the riff-raff'. Ironically, although the old proprietorial family trees have withered in the cold financial blast, the London branches of the two big unions remain firmly dynastic. Traditionally, they confine entry to 'the print', as they call it, to sons, nephews, cousins and other relatives, and this tight, clannish structure is what built up the chapels' formidable power. Many members of Sogat and Natsopa, with which it merged in 1981, in particular were drawn from the East End's post-Famine Irish community that also manned the tightly organised docks, as the names of such print leaders as O'Brien, Fitzpatrick and Brady testify.

The fact that production wages alone come to about a fifth of all a national newspaper's overheads – considerably more than total editorial costs – provides its own commentary on Fleet Street's crazy economic structure. The complex labour set-up, with three tiers of manual workers, regular staff, regular casuals (who have fixed days of employment and pension rights, such as they are) and 'casual' casuals who are 'on call' for shifts as needed, combined with a traditional system of 'blows' (rest breaks) and 'early cuts' provides a context for institutional featherbedding and fiddling unrivalled in any other industry. Most agreements stipulate a four-day week but in practice the majority work only three shifts totalling 25 hours, although paid for the notional 'week'. The 'blow' originated as a short breather for men working in hot pressrooms and stereotyping foundries but over the years has expanded into periods of up to half a shift which can be consolidated into time, even days, off which the employee can then work as a casual for another employer, say a Sunday paper, where he can get £130 for a 15-hour shift. The 'early cut' can mean virtually a token appearance in a heavily overmanned department: one process engraver of my acquaintance regularly worked shifts of only two hours. The combination of high incomes and a very short working week enables many print workers in Fleet Street both to set themselves up as proprietors in their own right, owning newsagents' and other shops, launderettes and taxis, and to take the time off to run them. One *Sunday Times* journalist, hailing a cab outside the paper's office in Gray's Inn Road, found himself being driven by a compositor with whom he had been making up pages the evening before.

The high degree of casual working offers almost unlimited scope for bunce and the 'old Spanish customs', as the more unorthodox work practices are known. In one year Sogat members may work more than 90,000 casual shifts in the machine-room area and 200,000 in the publishing department. The number theoretically employed in a department on any one night depends by strict agreement, on the number of pages the paper has decided to print. Officially, fathers of the various chapels are required to apply to the 'call office' of the union concerned for extra hands but in practice they may short-circuit the branch and give some of the shifts to friends or favoured members of their own regular staffs. And sometimes a chapel prefers to keep all the extra wages without bringing in any casuals. At one paper my appointment with a production executive was delayed while he dealt with an inter-union dispute. In accordance with the agreement, management gave the two unions concerned notice that the statutory number of casuals would be needed for a four-page increase in the size of the next issue. The readers, who correct the proofs, and belong to the NGA, agreed; the Sogat men, who read the original copy aloud to the readers, said they did not want to bring in any casuals but divide the extra wages among themselves. 'Now there's a row brewing between the unions that we'll have to settle somehow before we can get the paper out,' said the executive. For him it was a tiresome diversion from more constructive duties, but for the onlooker it was depressing evidence of both the fraudulent nature of much of the casual system and the greed that overmanning breeds.

Estimates of current overmanning vary from paper to paper. An estimate by the NPA (Newspaper Publishers' Association) puts it at 40 per cent overall. One manager calculated that the *Mirror* Group workforce could be cut by 50 per cent, with savings of £30m a year. Another put his two papers' potential savings at £25m. To illustrate the point, one director cited the manning situation in his paper's pressroom. 'The presses are completely automated and need practically no manual attention,' he said. 'Formerly we had 300 men running the old presses, now we have 200 but we could do the job with 60 – and that would be generous manning.' In the stereotyping department, with plastic plates replacing cast metal ones, 'eight men could comfortably do the work for which we pay 33'. Not the least bizarre fact of Fleet Street life is that many, if not most, of the craft union workers take home more pay than the journalists. Salaries of NUJ members on national papers – excluding senior editorial executives – are in the £17,500-£22,000 bracket, plus expenses, depending on the paper (the qualities tend to pay lower rates than the tabloids). An NGA member on piece work can make £30,000-£36,000, and some considerably more, and many on other rate systems can average £20,000 for three shifts. Not all manual union workers make such spectacular money: Sogat's lower-paid clerical and ancillary members – many of them women – bring the average closer to £15,000. The contrast in rewards for the people who write the paper and those who turn their copy into type is no recent phenomenon: before the last war, when the NUJ minimum for Fleet Street journalists was nine guineas (£9.45) a week, linotype operators were taking home £30. On the other hand, journalists have their own bunce in the form of 'built-in' expenses, money paid by agreement as a supplement to salary as distinct from actual expenses incurred covering a story. When Clive Thornton joined the *Mirror* Group as chairman-designate he discovered that the annual expenses bill exceeded £1m – more than the company's net profit. A check-up revealed that a high proportion of expenses sheets ranged from £8,000 to as much as £20,000 a year, 'many of the biggest claimed by people who never left the building'. When Thornton decreed that these must be halved within three months, for a start, the journalists' chapel pointed out that such a cut would abrogate agreements made with members who had been engaged on the understanding that they would receive built-in expenses related to their status. The amounts drawn as expenses are hardly a journalistic secret: Sogat clerical staff process expense sheets.

This awareness of the 'editorial rip-off', says Thornton, is regarded as a justification of their own bunce by other unions. Other justifications are harder to find. The linotype operators' high earnings have risen in inverse ratio to their performance. The once-high standards of typesetting have deteriorated sharply over the last decade as the growing rash of literals, misspellings, transposed lines and printer's pie testifies daily. And the level of proof reading has declined in parallel. One manager blamed it on the transfer of responsibility for recruiting to chapels: 'We are forced to take on people who are semi-literate – the union decides who is to be hired when there is a vacancy.' Many operators who retrain on the photo-composition keyboard have an even less sure touch. Fleet Street chapels have never allowed women near the hallowed keyboard, despite their superior dexterity: I can affirm from personal experience on a publication I edited, produced by a commercial printer, that female operators are both much quicker and more accurate, with hardly any mistakes in a column. These highly efficient women operators were former secretaries and typists who had recently been admitted to the NGA, it was suspected, more to keep up its numbers than because of any sudden conversion to the principle of sexual equality.

To the rare incomer from the outside world, Fleet Street's antiquated production system, byzantine wage structure, with maximum rewards for minimum skills, the shortest working week and the longest holidays (six weeks-plus) in industry, defy belief.

When Clive Thornton, who as chairman of Abbey National had injected catalytic new ideas into the building society movement, was appointed to mastermind the *Mirror* Group's proposed floating-off from its parent Reed International, he found 'a complete lack of union discipline bordering on anarchy'. The unions' concept of their power was rudely demonstrated when he invited the Employment Secretary, Tom King, to dinner at the *Mirror* offices to discuss the question of grants. In the middle of the meal the chief executive was called to the telephone; it was the father of the machine room chapel, who announced that his members strongly objected to the presence of a Tory minister in the building and that they would not be prepared to show him round. 'We should have been consulted before you invited him,' said the FoC. Overweening arrogance, perhaps, but it is as much a measure of management's past weakness as it is of the chapels' belief in their power to get things their own way. The truth is that Fleet Street's union indiscipline springs from the boardroom not the basement. To quote one senior management executive, 'The NPA is a joke'. The Newspaper Publishers' Association has never learned the lesson the unions have never forgotton: solidarity pays off. When the pressure is on, the chapels close ranks, the proprietors break ranks.

The NPA's lack of concerted policy and cohesive action dates from the ending of newsprint rationing in the mid-1950s, when Lord Beaverbrook virtually invented the 'ghost worker' to cope with the bigger advertising-packed issues of his booming *Daily Express*. The paper's machines could not print enough pages under existing union agreements so Beaverbrook's management arranged for the creation on paper of non-existent or 'ghost' machines to account for the longer runs on the real presses, with the existing workforce sharing out the extra wages paid out to the 'ghost' crews. The practice of buying off chapels by paying out, say, 100 wages to 80 men became standard and the ghost worker was soon an accepted feature of the labour scene, with men drawing a second or even a third packet in the name of Mickey Mouse, Gordon Richards of Tattenham Corner (the former champion jockey) and other celebrated figures, real and fictional, including even more brazenly that of Percy Roberts, then chairman of the *Mirror* Group, who revealed in 1978 that income tax investigators were inquiring into the practice. Not surprisingly, the tax men were unable to find any of the ghost workers at their equally fictional addresses. Roberts revealed further that when the *Mirror* made redundancy payments as part of a productivity deal 35 pay packets were left unclaimed, 23 of them in the name of Smith and the rest all 'Browns'. This, he said, was typical of the 'old Spanish customs' that govern Fleet Street and went on to explain these to his audience of provincial newspaper publishers. Naturally, in the interests of industrial peace, the national press itself did not report Roberts's revelations, but BBC Radio 4 looked into the subject, with limited success. No chapel official from Fleet Street would appear on the programme so an FoC had to be brought down from Manchester to explain the ghost system. Larry Lamb, then editor of the fearless *Sun*, prudently restricted himself to 'I am not entitled, I think, to discuss publicly internal matters of this kind which might aggravate a series of situations which are under negotiation'.

The Inland Revenue may have driven Mickey Mouse out of Fleet Street but the ghosts have not been totally exorcised. When a management audit at the *Mirror* revealed that one man was collecting four pay packets and this was drawn to the attention of the appropriate chapel father he replied: 'The company isn't losing anything – the manning agreement is for four jobs.' How many pay packets are the product of ghost manning and how many are achieved by other means is a matter of conjecture. A Sogat casual who was arrested 'on a minor matter' and found to have three pay packets, two from the *Sunday Times* and one from the *Radio Times*, was sentenced in 1982 to six weeks' imprisonment for falsifying wage dockets. The *Daily Telegraph* reported that a detective who made inquiries said in evidence that the fiddling of pay packets was 'a common practice in Fleet Street' and that the *Sunday Times* people were 'probably the worst of the bunch'. Times Newspapers, said the *Telegraph*, 'did not wish to comment'. Comment may be free, as the great C P Scott declared, but not when it comes to such delicate facts.

The next breach in the fragile unity of the NPA came, in 1955, when its 'one stop, all stop' pact, which stipulated that all papers would cease publication if one was prevented from appearing by unofficial industrial action, was abandoned after a month-long strike had kept the whole national press off the news-stands, with severe financial loss. Since then the sharpening edge of competition has meant that whenever a paper fails to appear, whatever the cause, its immediate rivals rush out thousands of extra copies to cash in temporarily on its difficulties with the added hope that some of the extra sales will stick: the circulations of both *Guardian* and *Financial Times* benefited significantly from the year *The Times* was shut down by dispute. A further loosening of the proprietorial bonds followed when the resale price maintenance legislation brought in by Edward Heath, then President of the Board of Trade, in 1964 ended price fixing by cartels. Up till then uniform cover prices for all popular papers and differentials for qualities had been established by NPA agreement. Now competition by price became the norm, with a brief interlude when Labour Prices and Incomes Board had to approve any rises. Today tactical pricing is a gambit used by both qualities and populars. Historically, *The Times* had always been the dearest of the three comparable national quality dailies, but Murdoch kept it pegged at an uneconomic 20p for over two years during which the *Guardian* rose from 18p to 23p, in a bid to reduce its increasing circulation lead. He also cut that of the *Sun* by 2p in 1981 to the same price as that of the *Star* to stave off its challenge at the lower end of the market and to undercut the *Mirror*. It is a costly and illusory tactic for populars, which make most of their money from sales – 1p increase adds anything from £3.5m-£9m in annual revenue, according to circulation. Within a year both tabloids had gone up to the *Mirror's* price.

What finally led to the emasculation of the publishers' union was, ironically, the so-called comprehensive agreements reached with the unions in 1968, in a despairing bid to sort out the industrial mess, but which have left its chairman, Lord Marsh – a former Labour junior minister turned company director, who took over the hot seat in 1976 – as impotent as the national leaders of the unions he negotiates with. The aim of the comprehensive agreements was to consolidate the numerous and fluctuating extras, including overtime, both actual and unworked, that comprised earnings and to rationalise the convoluted London scale of prices, with its bewildering permutations of piecework charges linked to such minutiae as the size, width and layout of type, into one overall basic rate, and, not least, to pare down the more outrageous overmanning. On the face of it, some of this was achieved, although in fact many of the manning cuts applied to ghost jobs. In return the individual chapels were able to get round the Labour government's wage controls, gain a more stable pay structure and, above all, secure the right to administer the agreed manning arrangements. In effect, the chapels could now run their own labour exchange; management had reduced its overseers' authority vis à vis the chapels and sold its hire and fire prerogative for a pricey mess of pottage. The touching belief that the new basic rate would solve the problem of increasing wage drift foundered on the self-interest that motivates proprietors as much as it does chapels. The NPA does in fact negotiate changes in the basic rate for all its members but a dozen other components are agreed by chapels direct with their paper's management, and these can double a man's earnings. 'The men regard the basic more as a retainer,' said a manager, 'a sort of down payment for turning up – the "fat", all the extras they have been able to screw out of management, on top of the basic, provide the bunce.'

The physical centralisation of the national press almost a century ago in virtually one street gave London's print workers a perfect base in which to develop and consolidate what Clive Thornton describes as their 'vicelike grip' on production. The national leaders of the print unions have had little real control over chapels since the first boom years and particularly since the comprehensive agreements came into force. 'Power lies on the chapel floor,' was how one manager put it. Two former general secretaries admitted privately to the writer that their Fleet Street members were virtually autonomous. 'There's not much you can do once they've dug their heels in,' said one. 'What is needed is stronger management.' To their credit, some previous leaders have tried to make their members face up to inevitable change. Three years ago Joe Wade, then general secretary, warned the NGA that it could not remain 'the last bastion of double key-stroking' (typing out again on the electronic keyboard copy already typed by journalists): 'Unless we are prepared to take on board the full implications of new technology and co-operate in improving productivity we shall be engulfed in a tidal wave of technology which we will not be able to control.' He pointed out that abroad, where direct input by journalists had been agreed, there had been no loss of printing jobs. It was a bold speech but it cut no ice with newspaper typesetters, least of all those in Fleet Street. The leadership's inability to get the chapels to toe the union line is frequently demonstrated in local disputes and was humiliatingly exposed twice on a wider front in the 1970s in abortive moves to introduce new technology in planned stages. The first attempt was in 1975 when the leaders of the (then) six unions got together and reached agreement on what *The Times* described as 'an unprecedented common approach ... on the modernisation of Fleet Street that might reverse the industry's declining fortunes'. The unions' policy document 'accepted that the more effective use of manpower at all levels and the introduction of new technology requiring a smaller labour force could be a contributory factor to reducing the production costs of national newspapers' and that 'rigid demarcation lines' could be modified if the employers agreed to appropriate compensation for voluntary redundancy, adequate pension schemes and retraining. A fortnight later the NGA chapels turned the proposals down flat. Exactly a year later, after exhaustive talks, the Joint Standing Committee for National Newspapers, comprising the leaders of the six unions and the managements of ten papers, produced another plan, *Programme for Action*, which envisaged a smooth transition to new technology and manning reductions in return for generous compensation and an agreed procedure for rationalising job demarcation. That too bit the dust, vetoed by the chapels, with the NGA men voting it down by three to one.

The NPA has never plucked up enough courage to force a showdown on the two sore points that managements complain about most, the automatic replacement rule, which has prevented any realistic slimming down of overmanned departments, and the absence of a lay-off clause that would act as a deterrent to wildcat stoppages by empowering employers to stop the pay of the rest of the workforce unless agreed dispute procedures had been complied with. 'You have no revenue coming in,' said a chief executive, 'the only saving is in newsprint and ink – you are lumbered with 80 per cent of your overheads and you never catch up on lost advertising.' The managerial side claims that the desired manning cuts could be achieved by well-compensated voluntary redundancy and 'natural wastage' because the Fleet Street production force has one of the highest age profiles in industry. In some areas like the composing room, stronghold of the NGA, and the publishing department (Sogat) it is estimated that nearly three-quarters of the men are over 40, with some veterans in their seventies soldiering on because a pensioner's income would hardly maintain them in the style to which they have become accustomed. The complexity of management's task can be gauged from the fact that a newspaper may have as many as 65 separate chapels to negotiate with. The *Mirror* Group, for example, has 30 chapel officials on its staff working full-time on union business: 'You pay them good money to screw you,' as a former manager remarked with feeling. Managements freely admit that the unions have them over a barrel. 'We are not proud of the fact that we so often seem to give in,' conceded a senior executive on a quality daily, 'but it takes a brave man to say 'no' an hour off press time, to a demand that may cost you £500. If we stood firm we could end up losing £250,000 or more. We can't sell yesterday's papers and the unions know that.' Few journalists would assert that Fleet Street managements are in the forefront of business administration, but it is undeniable that the brave – or desperate – 'no' can prove ruinously costly. In one (pre-Maxwell) four-day stoppage the *Mirror* Group lost £2.9m – more than its annual net profit. This summer the *Guardian*, which only recently achieved modest profitability after years of depending first on its Manchester *Evening News* and latterly on its enlarged chain of 32 local papers, lost all its London print in a five-day stoppage that 'maimed' the paper in the words of its editor, Peter Preston. The shutdown followed the loss of over a million copies during a two-month go-slow by 30 NGA stereotypers to press their claim for more than the 9 per cent increase offered. The stereotypers, who prepare completed pages for the presses, earn between £354 and £400 for an official four-day week (those on more affluent papers can make £700). Inevitably in such disputes, the paper loses income and the chapel gains some of its demands. Although the NGA agreed eventually to accept the 9 per cent, its members secured the incorporation of bonuses into the basic rate; in short, when the next pay annual rise comes round the percentage increase will be calculated on a higher base rate.

Whatever else, such disputes throw some light on the kind of money and overmanning that obtain in some departments. The *Financial Times*, which in 1983 lost £10m in a two-month stoppage by NGA members, last spring threatened to sue individual members of its NGA machine minders' chapel if they continued to disrupt production, with the loss of thousands of copies daily, in pursuit of what the chief executive described as 'an outrageously greedy claim'. He accused the chapel of stalling for 'days of futile masquerading as negotiation' before starting the go-slow. The machine minders, he said, were being paid £348 for a four-night week and the machine assistants (members of Sogat) got £304. In theory there should be 11 minders and 31 assistants on the presses each night; in practice there were as few as four minders and 15 assistants actually on duty. For this the NGA men were demanding an £80-a-week increase, while the Sogat assistants wanted another £70, plus increased manning. Or £18,000 a year for two days a week.

Both the main unions now have vigorous new young leaders who face fundamental problems about their memberships' roles, in relation both to the employers and to each other, as the first cold breakers of Joe Wade's 'tidal wave of technology' threaten to breach their once-impregnable monopolies. Tony Dubbins, 42, took over as general secretary of the NGA in 1984, and Brenda Dean, 41, at Sogat this year – the first woman to head a union in an industry where women have traditionallly been regarded as second-class citizens. In both unions Fleet Street membership is a relatively small segment, numerically, of their national strengths. Only some 20,000 of Sogat's 208,000 work for national papers – many are employed in the wholesale distribution side of the publishing industry – and the NGA proportion is even smaller, less than 7,000 out of 100,000. The two leaders face declining numbers, particularly in the commercial and book sectors, which have seen much of their trade driven abroad by high production costs, and the virtual elimination of the small jobbing firm by the photo-print process: although wages are well below Fleet Street's inflated pay packets, printers come high in the national table, well above the miners.

Since the 1960s the broad membership of the NGA has been gradually coming to terms with photo-composition: no commercial printer in the London area and few elsewhere of any size now use the hot metal process. But this sector of the industry has presented no real challenge to the union's control of the composing room, whichever technology is used, even if some jobs disappear. What the National

Graphical leadership is now desperately defending is 'its' newspaper keyboard from the threat of a takeover by the journalists. Recognising that attack is the best form of defence, it has been making a determined effort to infiltrate the editorial departments of the provincial newspapers, where the initial threat lies, and take over journalistic work with the bland claim that its members are merely, in the time-honoured tradition of their craft, 'following the work' – a euphemism for muscling in on the territory of the NUJ, retaining the right to negotiate wages and conditions for their members who retrain as journalists, and securing a foothold on the editorial floor that many NUJ members fear could turn into a stranglehold. This bid to assume editorial duties on the pretext that anyone who can tap a keyboard is an embryo journalist needing only a quick course in sub-editing or reporting to convert to full editorial status reflects the compositor's inherited elitism and strikes many journalists as a rather rich brand of *chutzpah*, coming from a union that has always regarded its own sphere as inviolable, even to the point where no sub-editor dare pick up a single slug of type to hand it to an NGA colleague (although here it should be said that personal relations are more matey than in most industrial contexts).

While not against some retraining of NGA transferees in principle, the NUJ is understandably wary of the Trojan horse ploy. Its difficulty is that it has never been able to secure the same closed shop rights that the other print unions established throughout the country years ago and its industrial clout is correspondingly much feebler. The NUJ has in fact closed shop agreements with ten of the national papers – the exceptions are *The Times* and *Sunday Times*, the two *Telegraphs*, the two *Mails* and the *Financial Times* – but even in the 'closed' offices the editorial chapels have rarely chosen to disrupt production to advance their claims like their more militant fellow unions, partly because the individualistic nature of journalism is less conducive to organised solidarity and partly because journalists tend to identify more strongly with the paper they write for, and therefore create, than manual workers who regard it rather as a place of employment. In the provinces, where almost nine-tenths of its 33,000 members work, NUJ negotiating strength is even less effective because not all journalists are members and a handful belong to the minority Institute of Journalists, which although it has only a tenth of the NUJ membership has pretensions to professional status which appeal to senior executives. Inevitably, this division of the editorial floor between two rival organisations is used by the NGA as a precedent that confirms its claim to bargaining rights in the journalistic field. The NUJ has been further handicapped in the defence of its sphere of influence by a power vacuum at the top this year following the resignation of its general secretary, Ken Ashton, after a dispute over the circumstances in which his pension rights were substantially increased. The affair, seen by some as a left-wing move to oust Ashton, split the union in a row that has left wounds which will not make the job any easier for Ashton's successor, Harry Conroy, a 42-year-old financial journalist from Glasgow's *Daily Record.*

NUJ anxiety about NGA motives is not unfounded. The National Graphical is itself a conglomerate, with a history of amalgamating with – ie taking over – other smaller or less powerful unions that mirrors the rise to a different kind of power of the proprietors it does battle with. Today's NGA is a composite of ten craft unions which have merged over the years under the leadership – some would say the domination – of the compositors in the interests of negotiating muscle. Its lineage is as diverse as that of a noble family but its genes show no comparable degeneration. The hard core of the NGA descends from the London Society of Compositors, which admitted only Londoners to membership and controlled all national newspaper typesetting until its merger in 1955 with the Printing Machine Managers' Trade Society under the title London Typographical Society. In 1964 the LTS amalgamated with the Typographical Association, which represented provincial compositors, to become a national body, as its new title proclaimed – National Graphical Association. Faced by the need for a united front and the threat to its numbers posed by technological change, it absorbed in quick succession: the Association of Correctors of the Press and the National Union of Press Telegraphists, 1965; the National Society of Electrotypers and Stereotypers, 1967; the Amalgamated Society of Lithographic Printers and Auxiliaries, 1968; the National Union of Wallcoverings, Decorative and Allied Trades, 1979; and the Society of Lithographic Artists, Designers, Engravers and Process Workers, 1981. It is a formidable combination and would have been a major force in an even more powerful grouping if the NGA's negotiations to merge with the NUJ had not foundered in fierce mutual recrimination in 1983. The NGA alleged that the NUJ negotiators did not represent the real views of its rank and file, but at the root of the breakdown was the NUJ's refusal to give up its tradition of open democracy in which all members can – although they rarely do – attend branch meetings and vote, in contrast with the NGA system of branch meetings attended by delegates elected by chapels – regarded by many journalists as a carte blanche enabling activists to manipulate the membership.

It is difficult not to have some sympathy with the compositors, on sentimental grounds, for the blow that photo-composition has dealt to their amour propre as inheritors of one of the oldest and proudest technical crafts in the world. To understand its dogged resistance to innovation one must remember that its roots go back to the introduction of printing into Britain by William Caxton in the 15th century when the first typesetters, including the monks, took over from the ecclesiastical clerks and the scriveners who practised around the churchyard of St Paul's Cathedral. As the first news-sheets began to appear in the 17th century and trade expanded, printers started to move down Ludgate Hill to Fleet Street. Already the compositors and pressmen were organised in 'chapels', each headed by a 'father' – names that may derive from the monkish connection but are first mentioned in print in a book called *Mechanick Exercises*, published in 1683. By the turn of the 18th century the chapels were uniting to form unions and developing the tight organisation which guarded jealously the high social status and rewards that a modern skill and full literacy conferred in an unlettered world. And to protect their monopoly from dilution apprenticeship was strictly limited, usually to relatives. The typesetters have always been reluctant to adopt any new techniques that threaten their craft standing or absolute control of the 'case', literally the wooden case in which the founts of type were kept. In the 1880s, when the newly invented Linotype was already in use elsewhere, the London newspapers continued to be laboriously set in handpicked type for half the decade until the union felt confident that it could control the job-devouring monster. Which it did for 70 years until the next monster entered the caseroom: this one was to prove much harder, perhaps impossible, to tame.

The severest blow to the NGA's hopes of keeping control of the keyboard and fending off the threat of direct input was dealt by Eddie Shah in 1983 when he invoked the Thatcher government's Employment Act of 1980 and defeated its attempts to maintain a closed shop by employing non-union labour at his Stockport *Messenger* Newspaper Group's works at Warrington after a six-month dispute which ended in often violent picketing involving 500 of its members. In the legal action that finally cost the union more than £700,000 in fines for contempt the judge said that the NGA had 'used its muscle to destroy the business' and had caused a 'most disgraceful near-riot involving several thousand people'. Later Shah was awarded further sums of £125,000 and £73,000 against the union for the harm it had done his business in what another judge condemned as 'a demonstration of mobocracy and intimidation at its worst'.

The real cost to the NGA, however, was not the money mulcted from it by the courts but the fact that Shah, an unknown small-time publisher of local free sheets, was now emboldened to step in where bigger operators had feared to tread and, with the law behind him, to take on the unions at national level. His now well-advanced plans for a national daily which he claims will be produced at a fifth of the cost of, say, the *Mirror*, sell at 17p and break even at a circulation of 300,000, through less dependence on advertising, involve no dramatic revolutionary techniques previously unknown to the newspaper world. What is new is that a British proprietor is prepared to defy the unions and put them into practice. The paper will have its editorial offices in Westminster, not Fleet Street, where journalists will type their copy straight into the photo-composition computer; facsimiles of the electronically-laid-out pages will then be transmitted by telephone line to five printing centres close to motorways and near major cities like Manchester and Birmingham as well as London itself; there copies will be run off in full colour and distributed within the area by franchised road transport. This system has two advantages: it will cut the present heavy distribution costs – in Fleet Street about 10 per cent of all overheads – and allow editions to carry last-minute news that comes too late for national papers printed the night before publication date.

Facsimile transmission is already used to a limited extent by those national papers which also print in Manchester but the number of pages sent by wire have been restricted by agreement with the unions, which insist on a certain proportion being made up 'live' to protect jobs. When the *Sun*, which prints all its four million copies in Fleet Street, unlike the other four tabloids, and has to fly 250,000 copies to Scotland daily, sought to open a plant there to print from facsimile, the plan was vetoed by the Scottish branch of Sogat, which also organises the typesetters as well as distribution and other workers. Facsimile is widely used in America where *USA Today*, the jazzy full-colour daily which is said to have inspired Shah's concept of a national paper, is beamed from Virginia by satellite to 14 printing centres throughout the US. Distance is no object: the Paris-based International *Herald Tribune* sends its pages by satellite to Hong Kong, where its Asian edition is printed. So far the only British paper using satellite transmission is the *Financial Times*, which started beaming its American edition to a New Jersey printing plant in July.

Shah's name is intoned by Fleet Street managements in the manner that 17th century mothers employed 'Oliver Cromwell' as an incantation to put the frighteners on their delinquent children, but there is a certain ambivalence about their welcome for the hero of the Warrington barricades: they see him as a brash outsider whose showdown with the NGA has wonderfully concentrated union minds, but there is an underlying worry that if his seven-day full-colour sheet does take off quickly next year it could siphon off advertising at his cheaper rates as well as circulation and inspire other mavericks to jump on his bandwagon before they too can break away from the Caxton heritage. But last July he struck a union deal which kindled new hope in managerial breasts and could yet have further-reaching effects on the whole Fleet Street economy than any success his paper as such may eventually achieve. It was, no less, a no-strike agreement between his News (UK) and the EETPU by which its electricians will become the sole union on his newspaper, completely excluding both the outraged NGA and Sogat. Within days Sogat struck back: Brenda Dean proposed a single-union agreement with Rupert Murdoch's News International at its new dockland printing site that would effectively shut out both NGA and electricians. It was against the background of this growing auction among rival unions, bidding against each other for exclusive takeover agreements that would give their members a monopoly in at least one group, that Robert Maxwell was able to force the NGA to accept his basic terms for a return to work after his recent 11-day suspension of the three *Mirror* titles and the threat that he would never again print them in Fleet Street. Selling the *Sporting Life* as part of the deal was no hardship for Maxwell, eager to be rid of its £3m losses and perpetual photo-setting troubles and faced with the coming competition of the new Arab-backed *Racing Post*. For once the NGA chapels saw that if they rejected the leadership's advice the writing on the garish *Mirror* building wall would be all too clear: not merely the *SL* jobs, but *all* the NGA's highly paid jobs and all the 'fat' would disappear into either a Maxwell subsidiary or the welcoming arms of a non-craft union with old scores to settle. Only one thing is clear as this book goes to press – newspaper industrial relations will never be the same again as rival unions abandon what little solidarity they shared in the rush to grab each other's jobs.

   In fact Shah's appetite for big-drum publicity has obscured the fact that the real drive towards full electronic newspaper publishing has come from the regional press, which has long been ahead of the nationals in technological innovation, using the photo-litho and colour processes that are still only a gleam in Fleet Street's bloodshot eye. As far back as 1983 the Newspaper Society, which represents the publishers of provincial papers, launched its Project Breakthrough campaign and warned the unions that it wanted a national agreement on full use of modern technology, including direct input by journalists and advertising staff by the following year, or some of its tougher members would go ahead anyway. They did so this year, in different parts of the country, with varying deals and '... or else' ultimatums that have split NUJ and NGA chapels from their respective HQs, with both journalists and compositors crossing picket lines, brought both unions into conflict with each other and set

Sogat against the NGA, which it suspects of seeking to 'steal' its tele-ad territory. It is a confused, complicated and rancorous situation in which only one thing is clear – the NGA is in retreat. On 15 July 1985 it surrendered its keyboard at the *Portsmouth News*, where for the first time on any NGA newspaper the journalists began to type their copy direct into the computer. In return the NGA was given a guarantee that there would be no compulsory redundancies, no loss of earnings and – to the dismay, if not fury, of the NUJ – that its members may join the editorial staff as sub-editors and retain NGA membership. Portsmouth is only a beginning: the Birmingham *Post* and *Mail* followed soon after with a similar deal. The chain reaction among provincial newspapers was under way.

Whether or not the one-union concept becomes reality – and its implementation would certainly bring new dimensions of disruption to the industry – the nationals are pinning much of their hopes on the transfer of their printing operations to the dockland sites three miles to the east of Fleet Street within the next three years. Murdoch's News International has already built a £72m printing plant at Wapping, near the Tower of London, for its *Sun* and *News of the World* production; the *Daily* and *Sunday Telegraphs* have a £75m plant going up on the nearby Isle of Dogs not far from a £15m installation planned by the *Guardian*. Associated Newspapers, publishers of the two *Mails*, are siting their £100m plant south of the Thames in the old Surrey Docks area. Robert Maxwell also plans to start printing on new colour presses in the dockland enclave within two years. The mass emigration involves only the presses and dispatach section – the editorial and typesetting departments will stay in Fleet Street and the pages will be transmitted by facsimile to the printworks. By this physical move the papers concerned will escape the time-consuming, frustrating congestion that hampers both the delivery of thousands of tons of newsprint and the distribution of the finished product via the narrow side streets and lanes of Fleet Street and be enabled at last to replace the worn-out 'bangers' with new modern presses providing both greater capacity and colour facilities. Not least, however, they hope that by transplanting the machine room and publishing workforce (largely Sogat, including many casuals) from the tight little enclave of Fleet Street, where offices – and cosy pubs – are a stone's throw from each other, making life easy for nomadic casuals, to the bleak and isolated waterfront, they will be able to cut manning significantly and wean the men from the fleshpots of EC4.

The hard-pressed *Telegraph*, for example, is looking for a cut of 500 jobs, mainly from Sogat but including a reduction of NGA strength from 320 to 190 as photo-composition is phased in, in return for a proper pension scheme and voluntary redundancy pay-offs of up to £45,000. The next step, it believes, must be the introduction of the long-sought 'no automatic replacement' clause to complete the slimming process. But not all managements are sanguine about the cordon sanitaire effect of the move. 'Dockland,' said a veteran manager, 'is only the far end of Fleet Street ... it won't be that easy.' News International has already found that out: its Wapping presses have stood idle for a year, with no union agreements in sight. Nor, at the time of writing, has any other paper got anything in writing yet. Whatever deals are eventually struck with the provincial press, where chapels operate in relative isolation and alternative jobs are hard to find, they will not necessarily set the pattern for the nationals, with their militantly autonomous chapels. Brenda Dean, Sogat's new leader, is regarded as 'a very tough lady who insists that all problems must be dealt with at national level', according to a managerial negotiator, but even she might find it as difficult to deliver as her predecessors, and her opposite number at NGA head office in Bedford, Tony Dubbins. Direct input, the logical conclusion of the electronic revolution, may be the norm outside London by the time the nationals have moved out to dockland, but it will have to remain a long-term hope rather than a short-term objective for Fleet Street's harassed managements. After all, the latest American equipment now being installed in several offices, the last word in sophistication, designed to enable journalists to carry out the whole photo-set operation, from setting copy to complete page make-up by keyboard, has had to be modified so that the comps may fulfil their anachronistic role.

Chapter 9

Public watchdogs or press lords' poodles?

> *Newspapers and periodicals serve society in diverse ways. They inform their readers about the world and interpret it to them. They act both as watchdogs for citizens, by scrutinising concentrations of power, and as a means of communication among groups within the community, thus promoting social cohesion and social change.*
> – Report of the Royal Commission on the Press, 1977

It can be argued – if with less and less conviction – that the country gets the government it deserves; only the more extreme right-wing critics of society and the manipulators of public power for private ends and their toadies in Fleet Street could pretend that Britain gets the press it deserves. At least the government is elected, even if by a system that represents the national will only in the crudest arithmetical terms, and there is the constitutional safeguard that it can be kicked out when enough voters in the right geographical locations decide they don't like what it is doing or just fancy a change. No such democratic, if imprecise, remedy applies to our newspapers: the irony of the tradition that the press must be free, in the Royal Commission's words, to act as 'watchdogs for citizens, by scrutinising concentrations of power', is that Fleet Street itself has become just such a concentration of power, personal power exercised by rich men who control the very instrument of scrutiny. The watchdogs have become press barons' poodles, yapping in support of their masters' views and commercial interests, barking against any threat to their undemocratic power.

How, then, in a society where public opinion is half-doped by the cultural soft drug of tabloid journalism, can we hope to spring the Catch-22 trap through the normal democratic processes? The honest answer must be: not very easily and not very quickly. For the problem of the national press is that its malaise is multi-dimensional and fraught with paradox in which a handful of proprietors have unrestricted freedom and newspapers *per se* have too little freedom within the framework of antiquated law to fulfil their classic role of disclosing whatever is desirable in the public interest, however unpleasant or embarrassing for governments of any colour, or organisations of all kinds, including trade unions, or companies, or members of the public themselves. The other, no less important, side of that coin is that the public itself lacks proper legal protection against the abuse of press freedom, whether under present circumstances or those created by future reforms which would enlarge that freedom in the public's own interest. Not least, at the material heart of the cultural-political-ethical nexus lies the whole question of the unstable economic structure which makes newspapers easy prey for the predators of the market-place.

Formidable though the dual task of democratising the press and making it financially viable may be, there has never been any shortage of proposals: government subsidies for the weaker papers and launch-capital grants for new ones, funded by an advertising tax on the Swedish model; a levy system that would redistribute profits from the more successful groups among the struggling titles; loan funds to finance modernisation and the rationalised sharing of plant, as in Holland; a national press corporation that would provide printing facilities at favourable rates to encourage new publications; regulations that would reduce overdependence on advertising by laying down the maximum percentage of its revenue that any paper could derive from that source; progressive levies that would make it financially less attractive to increase circulation over two million ... Some of the schemes work in other countries, some are patently Utopian or ignore the fluctuating nature of newspaper profits, if any, some are more likely to increase the number of bureaucrats than the number of titles, but all have been turned down, not merely by the three Royal Commissions since the war but by successive governments, including Labour, as either impracticable or – and here we come to the nub of the matter – too politically 'sensitive'.

The harsh truth is that while Labour, in opposition, never ceases to complain bitterly about the right-wing bias and concentration of ownership of national newspapers, in office it shrinks from any action that could be construed – by the press at least – as interference with the freedom that socialists know to be a sham. During the second Wilson government, when Labour had a majority of 99, two of his ministers underlined its unwillingness to grasp the nettle in the major debate that followed the damning exposure of the state of Fleet Street by the Economist Intelligence Unit mentioned in an earlier chapter. Said one: 'The government believe ... it is unquestionably for the industry itself to set about the task, which we do not believe to be impracticable, of sorting out its own economic difficulties in the light of modern conditions.' Another added: 'There is no possibility,

or at any rate no justification for direct government intervention ...
This kind of debate helps to bring to bear upon the press the pressure
of public opinion which helps it to solve its problems.' In reality this
kind of debate produces only a concerted whitewash by Fleet Street
that leaves public opinion uninformed about the true issues and
uncritically settling for the good old British status quo. Four elections
and two Fleet Street takeovers later, Labour's manifesto proposed
the break-up of the near-monopoly without actually spelling out how
this commendable intention could be implemented. Italy showed the
way in 1981 when it passed laws stipulating that no owner would be
allowed to control more than 20 per cent of the market and also
limiting the amount of the market that can be held by advertising
companies. Germany's monopoly laws also limit ownership: in 1982
its federal cartel office quashed a deal by which the huge and right-
wing Axel Springer group and another large company would have
secured control of more than 50 per cent of the national newspaper
and magazines market and dominated advertising in these fields.

But even on the Continent, where national newspapers form a
relatively small proportion of the total press, the breaking-up of near-
monopolies has proved easier to plan than to put into practice. Last
year France's socialist government enacted sweeping laws designed
to reduce the concentration of ownership by limiting any proprietor's
holding to 15 per cent of the circulation of 'all national daily papers of
that nature' (a national paper in France is defined as one with at least
20 per cent of its sales outside the metropolitan area) and a chain of
regional and local papers whose total circulation does not exceed 15
per cent of all sales in that field. To supervise this Press Act of 1984
President Mitterrand appointed a high-powered Pluralism Commission. The move was clearly intended to bring about the dismantling of
Robert Hersant's 35-strong publications empire, the biggest in
France, headed by his three right-wing Paris dailies, *Le Figaro*,
L'Aurore and *France-Soir*, which have taken a strong anti-Mitterrand
line. In the event, the law has become a dead letter. As the socialist
government fights for survival Hersant remains intact, waiting for the
return of a more sympathetic regime.

France's experience provides an ominous analogy for similar
counter-monopoly measures in Britain, where the magnitude and
highly concentrated nature of the national press would present
Labour with even stiffer problems. In terms of cost-effectiveness the
ideal publishing combination comprises three papers, a daily, an
evening, and a Sunday, ensuring maximum use of plant and
deployment of workforce. At the moment only one group owns more
than three nationals, Rupert Murdoch's News International, which
controls two sets of two, both comprising one daily and one Sunday,

The Times and *Sunday Times*, produced at one site, and the *Sun* and *News of the World* produced at another. When the latter two move to the dockland site Murdoch proposes to add an evening paper, the *Post*, which will go for a *Sun*-type readership uncatered for by the London *Standard* and rationalise the overheads of the new plant. This, on paper at least, would render the Murdoch empire ripe for 'demerging': the highly profitable *Sun-News of the World-Post* trio as one grouping and the Times Newspapers plus education supplements element, which barely makes a joint profit, as a separate entity. The latter could be sold off, given stiffer new monopolies legislation – and preferably to a consortium, or two consortia, of editorial and management staffs with bank backing, as envisaged by the papers' employees before Thomson went over their heads and sold out to Murdoch.

However desirable, though, dismantling the other giants would not be easy. Robert Maxwell's two *Mirrors* and his proposed London evening paper would constitute an economic unit, but a detached *Sunday People* on its own would not. And the *People*, after all, is one of the only three Labour-inclined papers in Fleet Street: there could be no guarantee that a new owner, consortium or otherwise, would keep it that way. The question is even trickier to resolve in the case of the other groups. Viscount Rothermere's Associated Newspapers, owning two nationals, the *Daily Mail* and the *Mail on Sunday*, one provincial morning, 13 provincial evenings and 32 local weeklies, all true-blue Tory, looks an obvious candidate for break-up. But the two nationals do not make a joint profit – the *Mail on Sunday* is estimated to be losing £18m a year – and they depend on support from the provincial chain and the parent group's North Sea oil and other diversified interests. A further complication is that local weeklies in the chains owned by Associated and Viscount Cowdray's S. Pearson & Son, parent group of the *Financial Times*, face increasing competition from giveaway sheets, which last year overtook the paid-for papers in total advertising revenue – £224m compared with £223m. While the national paper sector of Lord Matthews's Fleet Holdings group, comprising the *Daily Express*, *Sunday Express* and *Daily Star*, last year made a modest profit, slightly more than its Morgan-Grampian magazines, this came largely from the *Sunday Express* and the Group's £100m-plus stake in Reuters. The *Star* makes a loss but it helps to spread the newspaper operating costs. As a group, Fleet may be a potentially good buy for other expanding publishing companies like United Newspapers but the individual papers, demerged separately, would not make economic sense under present production conditions.

On the more constructive side there have been recent proposals for a media enterprise board, accountable to Parliament, which would provide launch capital for all kinds of new publishing initiatives and encourage consortium – as distinct from single proprietorial – ownership through low-interest loans. A new tax on media advertising, similar to those operating in some European countries, would contribute to Exchequer funding of the board. The scheme has the commendable merit of trying to counter the power of the conglomerate chequebook, although in practice it would bristle with potential difficulties, from the thorny problem of establishing a board that would be acceptable to successive governments to the tricky question of impartiality in deciding which applicants would get launching help, how much and for how long. If not pie in the sky, it has something of the flavour of pie on the distant horizon.

The real question is the blunt one that must be faced by political realists: what are the chances of a Labour government getting back in the near future in sufficient strength and with the toughness of will needed, in the face of the massive de-Thatcherisation programme necessary to reorient Britain, to push such a radical measure through Parliament in the face of a bitterly hostile press? It gives a socialist no pleasure to admit that market forces themselves are more likely to produce at least a partial answer sooner, limited initially perhaps, and gradual, but which could lead organically to the diversity essential if the high-minded prescription at the beginning of this chapter is ever to be implemented. Although the impact of the new technology on newspapers is proving a bitter experience for the print unions concerned, the wider truth is that their failure to come to terms earlier with the inevitability of change has exacerbated the inherent instability of an industry over-reliant on the fluctuating flow of advertising revenue and left it wide open to entrepreneurs whose sense of journalistic responsibility is in inverse ratio to their bankrolls.

Eddie Shah the union-breaker may not strike one as any more attractive a prospect than some of the present press barons, and his much-publicised daily, when it appears next spring, may not do much to fill the gap between the tit-and-trash lightweights and the textual heavies, but one may hope that it succeeds for one objective reason: if it breaks even with a circulation of 300,000, on, say, a quarter of Fleet Street production overheads and a greatly reduced dependence on advertising revenue, it could prove as catalytic as Northcliffe's first *Daily Mail* of 1896 and lead the way back to the plurality that is the true nature of journalism when not distorted by Northcliffe's ha'penny economics. Mass circulations on the scale of our national papers are a post-war phenomenon resulting from the confluence of freak factors that do not apply in other comparable countries (e.g.

Hersant's three French nationals have a *total* sale of 800,000, less than half that of either the *Mail* or the *Express*) and need no longer apply here once the relationship between sales, production costs and advertising is rejigged. A rational economic basis that encouraged new groups of all kinds to venture into what until now has been the prohibitively expensive preserve of very rich men could eventually cure Fleet Street of structural elephantiasis, but it will take more than cost-effective technology to woo popular journalism away from the easy delights of guttersniping and keyhole coverage and face the rigours of real muckraking in the public interest and the responsibilities that go with reporting society to society.

Unlike its contemporaries in the United States and most European countries, the British press is hedged in by a thicket of legal constraints that have tamed the instinct and will to disclose all which is the bedrock of serious journalism. The obsessive, almost paranoic passion for secrecy that marks the Thatcher government has worsened the situation but the Fleet Street tradition of waiting for the news to turn up rather than digging for it dates from the early part of the century when the press first began to feel the full impact of England's repressive libel laws. In 1908 it cost Northcliffe's *Daily Mail* and his group of other publications about £5m in today's money for alleging that the Leverhulme soap firm had cornered the raw materials market to force up prices. Since that and similar cases British editors have considered that the services of a good in-house night lawyer to vet all proofs is the better part of valour when it comes to an exposé that could cost the paper not only a large sum in damages and legal charges but a great deal of time and energy preparing a defence and fighting it through a constipated judicial system that benefits the legal profession more than its clients. Two examples: a case involving the *Guardian* was concluded only recently after 11 years' litigation; last April the BBC paid a Harley Street slimming specialist £75,000 damages and a record £1.2m in costs in settlement of a libel suit arising out of allegations made in its *That's Life* programme, which specialises in investigative features. Only a small percentage of libel claims get as far as judgment – newspapers spend thousands of pounds a year settling out of court.

In such an inhibiting atmosphere investigative journalism is as rare in this country as left-wing leading articles in the *Daily Telegraph*. Under Harold Evans the pre-Murdoch *Sunday Times* established a considerable reputation for digging out the dirt that owed something to Samuel Johnson's aphorism about a woman's preaching being like a dog walking on its hind legs – 'You are surprised to find it done at all'. This is not to detract from the paper's long and courageous battle to reveal the truth about the tragedy of the Thalidomide children, an admirable demonstration of what a determined editor can do, backed by a proprietor like the late Roy Thomson, who never interfered in editorial matters (provided the paper made money). At the same time the much-puffed Insight feature too often read more like hindsight in which the sheer bulk of evidence was in inverse proportion to the importance of the target. Occasionally the tabloids risk their hand if the topic is 'human' enough, but it can be a daunting experience. In 1981 the *Daily Mail* ran a bold, well researched inquiry, in the best investigative tradition, into allegations that the Unification Church (the 'Moonies') brainwashed converts, broke up families and had political and commercial rather than religious objectives. The Moonies sued for libel but lost after a trial lasting 101 days when a High Court jury decided that the allegations were true, and after an appeal was turned down they were faced with costs of £800,000. Had the *Mail* lost it would have been a severe blow to a paper that relies on the supporting profits of its diversified parent group. Although Fleet Street itself is physically in the City and only five minutes from the heart of the financial world, which has been rocked since the start of the decade by a series of major scandals at every level from fringe bank to Lloyd's itself, the reading public gets from its national newspapers only the most guarded and belated hints of the fiddles and frauds and the workings of the old-boy network 'arrangements' that can cost investors millions, until the cases come to court or an official inquiry reports and the story becomes virtually libel-proof. Only the readers of *Private Eye*, whose financial set-up makes it a less attractive target for the litigious, provides its readers with exposures in advance – often supplied by journalists whose own papers are not prepared to take a chance. It is noteworthy that while crime correspondents haunt Scotland Yard's press office for cops-and-robbers and Ripper-type copy few reporters bother to call on the City of London police, whose fraud squad works full time on the rising tide of sophisticated large-scale swindling.

Under a government that has shown it thinks the right to know is the prerogative of Whitehall, the pressure to keep the press in its proper place, below stairs, has been stepped up, as a few brief examples show. In 1983 it tabled the Police and Criminal Evidence Bill, designed to strengthen police powers for the more effective prosecution of professional criminals but which, if it had been made law, would have abrogated the journalists' traditional right to protect their sources by enabling police to seize confidential notes, files and records and empower magistrates to grant search orders and judges to demand that sources be identified. Only after a campaign of protest led by the Press Council, the NUJ, the Guild of Newspaper Editors and the Newspaper Society did the Home Office retreat and agree to modify the offending clauses. This right to withhold confidential sources, basic to the journalist's trade, was given statutory force by Section 10 of the Contempt of Court Act of 1981, but it did not save the *Guardian* from humiliating surrender when the government demanded that it return a memorandum from the Defence Minister, Michael Heseltine, to the Prime Minister, giving the date of the arrival in Britain of the first cruise missiles, which had been leaked anonymously to the paper by Sarah Tisdall, a junior civil servant, in 1983. The government did not use the Official Secrets Act section relating to classified material but claimed the document as its property and copyright. As a result the High Court sidestepped the provisions of Section 10 of the Contempt Act, which the *Guardian* believed would protect its source, and ordered the return of the memorandum on the grounds that it was government property, despite the fact that it would identify the person who leaked it, 'because the threat to national security lies in the fact that someone, probably in a senior position ... cannot be trusted'. The *Guardian* decided, rightly or wrongly, that it had no option but to return the memo because refusal would have resulted in contempt of court which, as had just been demonstrated by the industrial battle between the NGA and Eddie Shah (referred to in the last chapter), could have attracted punitive fines that might have crippled the paper.

This neurotic defensiveness of a government with an overwhelming parliamentary majority, but fearful of any leak, however technical, that might give the press a twig to beat it with, has been underlined by its recent use of the discredited Section 2 of the Official Secrets Act, which covers every sheet of paper, however innocuous, churned out by the prolific beaureaucratic mills of Whitehall. Although it tactically refrained from employing the Act against the *Guardian*, it had no compunction about using it against both Sarah Tisdall, who was sent to prison for six months as an 'example', and her fellow civil servant, Clive Ponting, who was found not guilty by a jury that made legal history by rejecting the judge's dictum that the interests of the government were the same thing as the interests of the state. The contempt laws as they apply to the press were originally conceived to guarantee all accused a fair trial unprejudiced by any revelations or editorial comment, and in that sense they are a safeguard of the citizen's right to be considered innocent until proved guilty. In 1949 Silvester Bolam, then editor of the *Mirror*, was jailed for three months and the paper fined £10,000 for contempt when it in effect found John Haigh, the acid bath murderer, guilty before his trial. Britain's strict *sub judice* rule may irk some journalists but it is a valuable instrument of judicial fairness that is denied to accused in America and some European countries where trial by headline is standard newspaper practice. But the contempt law as a potential secondary weapon to secure compliance in circumstances where an editor has been trapped by legal action that negates the journalist's right to protect his sources is hardly an advertisement for British justice.

If the national press is ever to become mature enough to fulfil its proper role as watchdog, critic of authority and those who wield financial power, promoter of social change and racial harmony and reflect the diversity of opinion of the community as a whole, a sweeping radical change in our archaic and repressive laws will be as essential as the modernisation of the technical processes of communication. The most obvious and crying need is for a Freedom of Information Bill, similar to those of the United States and Sweden, which would give both press and public a statutory right of access to all official information not involving national military or economic security. The Thatcher government flatly rejected the idea of such a bill as 'inappropriate' in 1983 but it has overwhelming support from a wide cross-section of informed opinion, ranging from politicians to senior civil servants and prominent lawyers. The Labour Party voted for its introduction at its 1981 conference and Lord Scarman, the distinguished judge, made a forceful plea for one in his Granada Lecture, 'The Right to Know', last year when he declared that the right to obtain information was too important to be left to the discretion of a minister, the civil service or a judge. "A free democratic society', said Scarman, 'requires that the law should recognise and protect the right of the individual to the information necessary to make his own choices and decisions on public and private matters, to express his own opinions, and be able to act to correct injustice to himself or his family.'

The value of a Freedom of Information Act to an open and confident society has been illustrated repeatedly in the United States since it legislated for access to official files in the mid-1970s: newspaper revelations resulting from this access have exposed the full horror of the My Lai massacre during the Vietnam war, the CIA's unlawful surveillance of the activities of American students, the harassment of political groups by the Federal Bureau of Investigation, the federal government's failure to meet its statutory obligations for the disposal of nuclear waste, an official cover-up to hide health hazards involved in atomic bomb testing, to name only a few of the better-known examples. The corollary of such a freedom act would be the long-delayed abolition of the Official Secrets Act. Over a decade ago the Franks Committee recommended its repeal and the replacement of its catch-call provisions by a new, more specific act that would protect a more limited range of sensitive government information, but it still stands on the statute book as a barrier to the citizens' right to know what is being done in their name and with their money, despite explicit condemnation from jurists of the stature of Lord Scarman and Lord Denning, former Master of the Rolls, and the admission of the Attorney-General, Sir Michael Havers, after the Tisdall and Ponting trials, that 'it is too widely drawn . . . in that, I think everyone is agreed'.

Another out-of-date law that will have to be modified, if newspapers are to be allowed to make news that is in the public interest by disclosing serious misdemeanours or situations without fear of ruinous law suits, is that of defamation, based on the medieval concept that a person's wounded reputation can be healed – usually several years after the event – by large sums of money. Here again the US has shown us the way. In the 1960s America's Supreme Court decreed that to protect the press's right to criticise officials and public figures and ensure free discussion of important issues in the public interest that anyone in those categories who contested allegations would have to prove 'actual malice'. Further, it laid down that the burden of proof now lay with the person suing, not on the defending publication, as in this country.

The difficulty in proving malice has both reduced the number of libel suits in the US and resulted in journalists winning the great majority of those actions that are brought to court. Here, it should be pointed out, the demand for a reform of Britain's punitive libel laws is not confined to journalists or left-wing politicians. In 1970 Sir Peter (now Lord) Rawlinson, QC, then Attorney-General in the Heath government, told Parliament that reform was called for because 'it is lawyer's law . . . made mostly by the judges . . . there is unfairness and a restriction of the right of free expression . . . we should eliminate all the complications arising from the defence of fair comment and the element of malice that must be introduced'.

When a government does face up to the formidable task of initiating such radical reform – and it will take not only political guts but more than one term as well as a commanding majority to impose such fundamental changes on a legal profession steeped in the obscurantist tradition of case law – the press will in its turn have to offer more than one *quid pro quo* to the public whose interest it claims to defend. Journalists cannot have it both ways. To balance its new right of access to official sources there would have to be a Privacy Bill on the lines of the one enacted by the United States at the same time as its Freedom of Information Act. This would provide legal protection against intrusion into private lives where no question of the public interest is involved and would outlaw the harassment of people caught up, however indirectly, in what the tabloids consider hot stories. The omens, it must be confessed, are not propitious. Several bills embodying the privacy principle have failed to get through Parliament since the war. An exhaustive inquiry in the 1970s into the question by Justice, the British section of the International Commission of Jurists, recommended legislation 'to provide a civil remedy for any substantial and unreasonable infringement of any person's privacy, while fully safeguarding the interests of the community, and especially the needs of the press as a guardian of the public interest'. It got a bad press. Most editors react strongly to the idea of such curbs, citing the barrier to investigative journalism (*sic*) they could create, and the Press Council itself handed down its own judgement in 1971 in a memorandum on the subject: 'Legislation to protect privacy so far as the press is concerned would, in effect, transfer responsibility for the maintenance of journalistic standards to the courts and would represent a complete reversal of the policy studiously followed by successive governments of leaving the question of standards to the authority of the Press Council.' The pious principles enunciated in that document were already badly frayed when it was published; today they are even more academically unrealistic as journalistic standards slip steadily down the probity scale and the Press Council's moral authority disappears, like its Declarations of Principle, into editorial wastepaper baskets. The Council's latest report, for the years 1982/1983, reveals that the volume of complaints has gone up dramatically to 973, a 25 per cent increase in the second year. What it does not say is that this total is more than double the number dealt with annually in the 1960s and 1970s. The report also attacked 'improper pressures exerted against editors and journalists' and cited examples of the 'abuse of power' involving proprietors, advertisers and trade unions. On the positive, more hopeful side, the NUJ drew up plans at its 1985 annual delegate meeting for the establishment of a new Ethics Council to police its code of conduct. This body will deal with complaints about any work or behaviour of NUJ members accused of contravening the code by other members or branches of the union or by members of the public. It will be able to recommend fines, suspensions or expulsions to the NEC. While this belated move to give ethics a place alongside wages and conditions on the agenda must be welcomed, it has to be said that the union's record on ethical issues in the past has been depressingly feeble, not least because its disciplinary influence is weakened by the fact that not all journalists belong to the NUJ.

The second, and equally important, right that a really liberated press will have to offer the public is the right of reply, a common feature of press law in other European countries. Past criticism of the popular press has often centred on the sleazy character of its gossip columns, prying into the marital and extra-marital affairs and sexual proclivities of 'celebrities' and paying their cocktail circuit narks for any dirty bedlinen that can be washed in public. Admittedly, their prurient disclosures are hardly what Delane had in mind, but the concentration of critics on the bedroom branch of junk journalism is a diversion from its more serious aspects. For one thing, gossip has been a staple of all levels of journalism since 1704 when Defoe spiced his brilliant, polemical *Review* with as much personal scandal as he could lay his gifted pen to, and it won't go away; for another, most of the 'names' whose antics are chronicled by the Nigel Dempsters of this world, or rather demi-monde, are the very people who are celebrated only for appearing in gossip columns, and the others, such as members of the royal family and their hangers-on, and the titled and millionaire classes, have PR minders to ensure *their* right of reply. The people who need protection from the Wolfe pack are ordinary citizens with no resources to counter untrue or distorted reports, whether inspired by malice or bias or failure to check, which can ruin reputations and threaten livelihoods or simply hold them up to contempt, humiliating ridicule or worse, as in the case of racism. These are the people I had in mind when I first advocated the adoption of a legal right of reply in the columns of the *New Statesman* in the 1960s and then, four years ago, as a member of the Labour Party's Media Studies Group, proposed that the party should include such legislation in its next manifesto (which it subsequently did).

Although nearly 40 per cent of the complaints against papers upheld by the Press Council over the years concern the failure to publish replies or corrections, or editorial alterations which fudge these when they are printed, it has consistently rejected the principle of a statutory right of reply. Perhaps the best indication of the potential value of such a right to individuals or organisations who are seriously misreported, misrepresented or maligned is the unanimous condemnation of the idea by editors whenever the 'threat' surfaces. In 1982, when Frank Allaun, then Labour MP for East Salford and a doughty campaigner against media excesses and bias, was given leave to introduce a Private Member's Bill, I collaborated with him in drafting one to 'give members of the public the right to reply to allegations made against them or misreporting or misrepresentations'. Not only did Allaun's bill fail to get a second reading because too many Labour MPs – including several who are members of the NUJ – failed to appear in the chamber for the vote, but it was universally savaged by the qualities as well as those populars that could spare the space to mention it. The line was predictable: not only would such an act be an unacceptable interference with the editor's independence (*sic*) but unworkable as replies flooded in from every crank in the country and filled up valuable editorial space (*sic*). Even the *Guardian* descended to pejorative dismissal: 'High principle ... low farce ... mare's nest of barren argumentation ... ' although it conceded, uneasily, that 'there is no means of shifting a perception that will sooner or later find expression in the Statute Book'. With unconscious but appropriate irony several critics, including the journalists' trade paper, the *UK Press Gazette* (then under different owners and editor), misrepresented some of its key clauses. The bill, drafted with some haste to meet the parliamentary deadline, may have lacked the precision which Fleet Street demands of its leader writers but it followed the outlines of established Continental practice and was sponsored by equal numbers of Labour and Conservative Members, including both journalists and lawyers. It proposed that replies to factually inaccurate or distorted reports be printed within three days of receipt by the editor concerned, in the same position and up to the same length as the original. Complaints disputed by the editor would be referred to a panel of judicial status comprising representatives of the public, journalism, media management and trade unions, presided over by a judge. Where a complaint was upheld the editor would be required to publish the reply within three days of receiving the panel's judgment or be liable to a fine of between £2,000 and £40,000, according to the seriousness of the offence.

Almost all European states from Norway to Greece have versions of France's Droit de Réponse, which dates from 1881, but in most of them the diversity of newspapers catering for a wide range of views and tastes and an awareness of the law that tempers their approach means there is only occasional recourse to the right of reply machinery. To take just one example, West Germany, where each Land administers its own version of the press laws. Its biggest paper, Axel Springer's right-wing *Bild*, with a circulation of five million, prints some 50 'counter-statements' from complainants each year – hardly the avalanche feared by Fleet Street. In Hamburg, for instance, a special media panel of the Landgericht (state court) deals with an average of 100 cases a year, half of which are won by complainants, who are given an enforceable court order obliging the publisher or television station to print or broadcast their counter-statements. Only corrections of fact are allowed and these may not be longer than the report complained of. The right of reply is open to both individuals and organisations which claim to have been seriously misrepresented. If the right of reply can work routinely without fuss in Germany need it be such an unthinkable concept in a Britain whose newspapers are so vehemently in favour of law and order? For if British editors could see beyond their prejudice they would realise that, properly administered, the right of reply has a double merit: it would rationalise the libel situation by providing genuine complainants with immediate and almost cost-free redress in place of long, burdensome law suits; and it would extend such redress to people – that is, most of the public – who cannot afford to bring an action for defamation.

Whatever one's views about the causes and possible cures, the British press is fast approaching a watershed that is fraught with both dangers and new opportunities to revive its tarnished reputation. On the plus side, there is the gradual move into the era of electronic publishing which, if rationally co-ordinated by realistic agreements, could in the long term, by its impact on both initial capital costs and overheads, bring about a gradual return to the diversity essential to an informed, socially balanced and politically literate democracy. New technology, used to full capacity, could open the way for new titles like the proposed TUC-backed Labour paper – a non-starter under present conditions in terms of the launch fund of £6.7m envisaged in 1983, but perfectly feasible if the newspapers' economic base is revolutionised. After all, Shah's much more ambitious project is planned to take off on an initial investment of £18m – peanuts by national paper standards. Against the qualified optimism such developments may inspire, one must range the built-in realities of the Fleet Street ethos that will not be reformed in the short, or even the medium, term by the micro-chip alone: its domination by a handful of tycoons; the vulnerability of the minority of papers which depend for their continued existence on their financial success as newspapers in an unstable market; the alternative 'security' that goes with the patronage of a conglomerate millionaire and its price – the inevitable erosion of editorial independence; the continuing decline in journalistic standards as competition intensifies for a diminishing share of the national advertising expenditure – a trend that could worsen rather than improve, in the short term, when new-style nationals à la Shah challenge the tabloids with much cheaper rate cards. Nor is there any guarantee that when established papers begin to benefit from the substantial savings resulting from the new technology and realistic manning, plus the millions to come from their Reuters holdings, that they will plough the profits back into improved editorial coverage, at home and particularly overseas, rather than spend it on even bigger bingo prizes and more TV advertising campaigns as reader bait.

Plainly, the free-for-all that passes for freedom in the Tory market forces philosophy has no comprehensive answer to a multi-faceted problem that demands solutions beyond the scope of diligent management and marginal profit. Equally plain is the inherited dislike and suspicion of the law that colours the press's attitude to any suggestion that constructive legislation could make for better journalism. Smug in the conviction that such formulations are for foreigners without benefit of Magna Carta, Britain has always set its face against any system of codified law. As so often in its relationship with the European Community, which Fleet Street unanimously and relentlessly advocated as the remedy for all the nation's ills, Britain is odd man out: this country is the only one in the EEC without a written constitution and the only one without the press laws that form one of its most important guarantees of freedom of expression. It is surely time, if British journalism is ever to acquire any integrity, to confront the need for a comprehensive law or charter that would define both its rights and its responsibilities in relation to the specific laws, present and future, affecting its function and conduct – libel, contempt, freedom of information, right of reply, privacy – and provide a legal framework establishing, *inter alia*:

- safeguards for the independence of editors and their protection from improper pressures from proprietors, advertisers, trade unions and other organisations
- the incorporation of a code of conduct based on that of the NUJ
- the investment of a reformed Press Council with statutory power to impose appropriate fines on newspapers that knowingly breach the code of conduct
- the appointment to the boards of all national newspapers, popular and quality, independent directors without whose approval editors cannot be engaged or dismissed
- machinery for the consultation and involvement of editorial staff in the appointment of editors
- the appointment to all national newspapers of an ombudsman/ woman, on the North American model, to monitor and to attempt to settle routine complaints from the public to obviate unnecessary resort to the Press Council or Right of Reply Panel
- the reference of all newspaper takeover bids to the Monopolies Commission for full examination of the circumstances, with special reference to applications from editorial-management consortia of the publications involved
- the restriction of ownership of national newspapers and their control, direct or indirect, to persons of British nationality and companies or organisations whose headquarters are registered in the UK
- regulations requiring that all national newspapers and periodicals be made available on demand throughout the national distribution network.

To ensure continuity under governments of differing complexion, the press laws would be overseen by an independent press authority, operating on the 'arm's length' principle, on the lines of the Independent Broadcasting Authority. Such a body would be much less expensive to set up and to run than a board providing grants and subsidies and would be less subject to the political pressures involved in the disbursement of Treasury funds.

Looked at dispassionately from the broader perspective of a public that – largely through the influence of television – is becoming more and more concerned with developments affecting the quality of life (the rape of the environment for private gain; growing pollution, the indiscriminate use of hormones in animal breeding for bigger, quicker profits; and the substitution of chemical 'additives' for natural nutrition) society's tolerance of the parallel adulteration of its major supply of news and information, the basic source of a country's democratic health, would be astonishing if one did not not recall the Catch-22 situation which leaves the press itself as judge of its own case and censor of the complainants' evidence. 'We are only giving the readers what they want,' runs the argument of tabloid editors and their owners when challenged about their more disreputable activities. 'If they didn't like our kind of paper they wouldn't buy it.' In the first place, such justification smacks of the sophistry of the drug pusher and porn pedlar who encourage a debasing or pernicious habit and then cater for it, and it is alien to the spirit of honest journalism. In the second place, it dodges the fact that ordinary readers who find the qualities too rarified for their taste have been left with no reasonable choice. And the audiences for intelligent television programmes – 11 million viewers watch the BBC's *Question Time*, in which Robin Day and a panel discuss the serious issues of the hour, and nine million see ITV's *World in Action* programmes on important themes – show that their taste is markedly superior to that of the tabloid back benches who decide what they will be served up with their breakfast the following morning.

In an imperfect world, legislation is admittedly no cure for all its ills, or theft and murder would have gone out of fashion, but it can be a deterrent and the agent of vital change. A press charter, if a future government will summon up the mettle to challenge Fleet Street on its own midden, might not give the British public the press it deserves but it could lead to the evolution of a press that deserves more respect.

Complaints upheld by Press Council over 15 years, 1969-1983

Dailies

Daily Mail 34
Daily Express 24
Sun 19
Daily Telegraph 18
The Times 11
Guardian 11
Mirror. 7
Daily Star 6
Financial Times . . . .—

Sundays

News of the World 14
Sunday Times 11
Sunday Express. 11
Observer. 7
Sunday Telegraph. 5
Sunday People. 5
Mail on Sunday 2
Sunday Mirror . . . .—

Source: Press Council annual reports

Brief bibliography

Brendon, Piers: *The Life and Death of the Press Barons*, Secker and Warburg, 1983.

Boston, Richard (Ed.), *The Press We Deserve*, Routledge and Kegan Paul, 1970.

Chester, Lewis and Fenby, Jonathan, *The Fall of the House of Beaverbrook*, Andre Deutsch, 1979.

Christiansen, Arthur, *Headlines All My Life*, Heinemann, 1961.

Cleverley, Graham, *The Fleet Street Disaster: British national newspapers as a case study in mismanagement*, Constable, 1976.

Cudlipp, Hugh, *Publish and be Damned*, Dakers, 1953; *At your peril*, Weidenfeld, 1962.

Driberg, Tom, *Beaverbrook*, Weidenfeld, 1956.

Economist Intelligence Unit, The National Newspaper Industry, a Survey, EIU, 1966.

Evans, Harold, *Good Times, Bad Times*, Weidenfeld, 1983.

Ferris, Paul, *The House of Northcliffe*, Weidenfeld, 1971.

Hirsch, Fred and Gordon, David, *Newspaper Money*, Hutchinson, 1975.

Jenkins, Simon, *Newspapers, The Power and the Money*, Faber, 1979.

King, Cecil, *The Cecil King Diaries*, Jonathan Cape, 1972.

Leapman, Michael, *Barefaced Cheek, the Apotheosis of Rupert Murdoch*, Hodder and Stoughton, 1983.

Royal Commissions on the Press: 1947, 1961–62, 1977, HMSO.

Sisson, Keith, *Industrial Relations in Fleet Street*, Blackwell, 1975.

Taylor, A. J. P., *Beaverbrook*, Hamish Hamilton, 1972.

Williams, Francis, *Press, Parliament and People*, Heinemann, 1946; *Dangerous Estate*, Longmans, 1957; *The Right to Know*, Longmans, 1969.

Index

Other titles from Comedia